Grieving with Grace

By Stephanie L. McKenny

Grieving with Grace

ISBN: 978-0-9961018-6-8

Copyright © 2025 ~ J & J Publishing Company

A self-publishing company owned by

Stephanie L. McKenny

All rights reserved. No part of this book may be reproduced in any form except for the inclusion of brief quotations in a review, without permission in writing from the author or publisher. Biblical quotes throughout this book come from the King James Version.

References from The Holy Bible and Merriam-Webster Dictionary

Matthew 5:14

Blessed are they that mourn: for they shall be comforted.

2 Corinthians 12:9 a

And he said unto me, My grace is sufficient for thee: for my strength is made perfect in weakness.

Dedication

Dedicating this book to my father, mother and my daughter. Loving and remembering you all. Losing you all taught me something.

To those who have loved ones that have passed away and are having difficulty processing the loss. I hope this helps you to get through the grieving process.

Grieving with Grace
Contents

Transparency Moments 1
THE LETTERS 3
   Dear Crystal, ... 5
   Dear Daddy, ... 9
The Grieving Process Is Not Easy: 15
Help Me…Help them. 19
God's Strength 21
It Happened So Fast 23
The New Norm 27
Things are Birthed out of Pain 31
Standstill 33
Closure 37
Keep Going Don't Stop 41
Mother/Daughter Connection 45
Prayer 49
A Better Place 53
Out of My Hands 57
Counseling 61
Three Years turn to Thirty Days 65
1:23 a.m. 69
First Mother's Day 73
Mother/Daughter Tea 75
Triggers 79

LIVE	83
No Place Like Home	87
Don't Get Stuck in the Pain	91
Take Care of You	95
Call for Help	97
Accept It	101
Never Be the Same	105
Her Strengths	109
Support of Others	113
68	117
Advocate	121
The Cell Phone	125
Acts of Faith Tour	129
I was Angry	133
Stabilize Yourself First	137
Connected	141
Fifteen	145
Her Body is Tired	149
God Showed Me	153
Be the Bridge	157
Time is a Treasure	161
I Don't Like It	165
The Hospice Experience	169
A Chance to Love	173
Check on the Strong People	175
The Drive to Charleston	179
And She Loved You	183

The Last Conversation	187
One Year Later	189
The Emotions Resurfaced	193
Thoughts	201
When is she coming back?	205
Don't Burn Bridges	207
Friends	209
The Kitchen Table	215
I'm Okay	217
Valentine's Day	221
The Telephone Call	223
Missing Him	225
At Midnight	229
Granddaughter	231
The Triggers	235
Go by the House	239
Trip to New Jersey	243
Moving Clothes	245
The Comments	247
First Day of Chemo Memory	249
God Still Needs You	251
Daddy, You Did Well	253
GRIEF FACT SHEET	255
Stages of Grief	257
About the Author	259

Transparency Moments

After the passing of my daughter, I began to type these transparency moments on my social media page. It was my way of journaling and releasing my feelings. It helped me to process my feelings. Two years later after her passing, I found myself typing these transparency moments to share about my feelings about my father's passing as well. As I went through my grieving process, I was able to express my feelings and share some things I learned along the way. So, as you read each transparency moment it reflects what I felt that day, the lesson I learned ("It Taught Me") and/or the revelation that came to me from it. I have also included a few tips under the "Grieving with Grace" portion to help you move through your **GRIEVING WITH GRACE.**

My prayer is that this book will be a tool to help you navigate through this part of the journey of your life. In some of these writings, I also encourage you to write in a journal. Journaling is another way to help you through the process.

THE LETTERS

Sometimes during the grieving process, you may feel the need to write a letter to your loved one that has passed away. Initially, you may question the need to do this. After all, they are no longer here, and they won't be able to read it. However, the letter really isn't for them, but more so for you. It is a way for you to release some feelings, release any regrets, release yourself to apologize or even forgive them.

Writing a release letter can be very therapeutic and it can also help you to move on with your life. It can help you to bring closure if you feel you need to do so. Try it. It's totally up to you, but if you have some feelings, you didn't get a chance to express or you're feeling stuck in your grieving process…. write it. Journal it. Release it.

Dear Crystal,

I can remember the day that you were born so clearly. I was so young, and I really had no idea all that came with having a baby, much less about the responsibility of being a mother. I remember not knowing even how to put on your diaper. One of the nurses at the hospital had to show me how. I was only fifteen. I didn't even know who I was, nor did I have any clue of what was ahead of me. I must admit that I didn't know what to expect concerning you. Nor did I know that your life here on earth would only consist of 36 years. I had no idea that I would have to bury you.

I'm truly grateful to God I had very supportive parents who took you in as if you were their own. I would often tell people that we were raised like sisters. Earl and Marian (I say their names respectfully) were always supportive of us both and as many years passed by, I often thought their love for you surpassed their love for me. I can honestly say unconditional love was shown and felt by them.

Initially, Crystal, I did not want you. Not necessarily you per se, but the whole idea of being pregnant at 15 years old. I know that sounds crazy, but at 15 years old being a mother was a hard pill to swallow in the 80s. I can remember only one other girl in high school that was pregnant at the time. She was a senior and I was a freshman. Whew...when I look back now it was a lot. My parents suggested adoption prior to me delivering you. However, after Dr. Jones placed you on my chest, the bond was established. The night before it was time for me to be discharged, I can remember so vividly telling my parents that I could not put you up for adoption. I cried because my love for you had formulated. They understood my conviction and told me that we would all make it work. So, you went home with us to the famous "68." A place that you and I would forever call home. It was our safe place. A place that we often returned to until we couldn't any longer.

I know that you are gone, and I've come to accept it, but I will never forget you or the bond that we once shared. I'm writing this letter of release so that I can let go of some things that have been on my heart. When we moved to SC things changed for us. Situations occurred and words were shared that at times weren't so pleasant (IYKYK). Hindsight, I hated this for us because we wasted so much time being caught up in the differences between us. Along with listening to input from outside influences, we missed time to create new memories. You felt abandoned and at some point, I felt hated. I know now that it wasn't either of our intentions to hurt one another. You were looking for me and I was looking for you (how it started). For many years, I've lived with regret for my actions or lack thereof, but I've come to realize I can't turn back the hands of time. I've forgiven myself and forgiven you.

Today, I am thankful that we were able to reconnect our relationship shortly after your initial diagnosis. I missed you and I missed us and as you've shared…you did too. However, that reconnection was not long. Things happened so fast. I hated that you had to go through this pain. I had no idea the last day you would stop breathing would be at 1:23 am on December 2, 2018. A day I will never forget.

As I move forward, I will choose to remember you and us in a positive way. I will remember your laughter and the times we shared with each other. I will remember the hospital visits and how we talked and laughed so much that the staff wanted to find out what the laughter was all about during your most traumatic experience. I will treasure those moments.

I'll never forget you Crystal and I love you always.

Love, Ma

Dear Daddy,

I want to first say that you were such an amazing man. I miss you so much and I wish that you were here so I could sit with you to glean some wisdom. I think of you now and wish that I had done more of that. In my eyes you were such a strong man and as a young girl I can remember thinking that you could fix anything. This makes me smile because I remember this book you had, not quite sure of the name of it, that said something like, "Fix Anything in the House." And there were many times that you tried to do just that.

I want you to know that you were such a great father, a great grandfather and even a great-great grandfather. You were loved by many, and you displayed unconditional love. Not only towards me, but I noticed you shared it with those you connected with. You made others feel welcomed and appreciated.

I can remember being a little girl around the age of 6 or 7 years old and telling you that when I grew up that I wanted to marry you. I know now that it was impossible, but at that moment I must have seen something in you so special. Crystal and I used to say that when you were born, they broke the mold of creating good men (smiles). I love you so much, daddy, and I miss you.

I can remember you being such a good provider to our family. You made sure we had what we needed. Our yearly family vacation to Wildwood will also put a smile on my face. I'm glad you and I were able to go on your 80th birthday. I got a chance to visit it again, Daddy a few years ago and it felt so good to be there. I got to walk on the Boardwalk and hear, "watch the tram car, please" as it passed by with those riding on it. Every now and then I still think about those vacations and appreciate the experience. Those were such good times.

When I was looking through some of your papers, I came across an article about you that described you as a person with tenacity. The article was about your educational journey. You didn't have the finances to finish dentistry school because you had to take care of your family (me and mommy). You kept pushing forward and were later able to finish dentistry school and opened your office in November 1974 on Central Avenue in East Orange. There you remained until 2016. Wow! You were committed to what you loved to do. You followed your dreams and pushed forward even when the odds were against you. You didn't give up; you found another way to achieve your goal. I love you for that, Daddy. I think it's helped me push through obstacles I've faced on the path of my life.

I saw a strength in you that I have grown to appreciate and admire. Even through the losses that you experienced, even beginning when you were just eleven years old with losing your mother. You displayed a strength that I'm sure you couldn't even explain when my mother passed away. I know you mentioned that the two of you were high school sweethearts, and you stood by my mother during some of her tough times battling mental illness. I never knew the real story of what happened to my mother prior to me being born, but when I found out I cried. For some reason I felt her pain. I admire and appreciate you for being strong enough and loving her enough through it all.

When I left New Jersey, you still at times would send me special gifts and money. I appreciated that so much. I hated that I didn't visit as often when I first moved. I was trying to adjust, but I'm thankful that you and mother continued to help with Crystal. I appreciate you loving her the way that you did. I want you to know, I honor you, Daddy. You are the best father that a daughter could ask for. No one can change that perspective, and they better not try (smiles). You did well, Sir. I miss you so much. I hope you forgive me for my mistakes, and I truly hope I am making you proud. Love you forever, Daddy.

Love, Stephanie.

TRANSPARENCY MOMENTS

Transparency Moment – January 22, 2019
The Grieving Process Is Not Easy:

This grieving experience is not a pleasant one. For anyone grieving I realize it's very hard at times. I'm not even going to sugarcoat it one bit, it's hard. Sometimes the tears come at any given time. The tears are coming even as I write this.

However, God can heal the pain and brokenness. He can help fill the emptiness inside. It's never God's intention for us to stay in a painful state. I've come to realize there is nothing anyone can do to bring my daughter back.... NOTHING. You may have come to realize that as well and have accepted it. No one can bring your loved one back physically, but they will always be in your heart and a part of your life. Memories and good times will NEVER be removed from your heart.

It Taught Me

With that being said, for those people who remain in your life, make sure you spend time with your loved ones, repair broken relationships, FORGIVE and LOVE AGAIN. Don't allow anything to separate you from those you love.

During my process of grieving, I am thankful for the amazing people that God has been sending in my life to make sure I'm okay.

I can't emphasize enough about the importance of spending time with those you love. Don't allow petty drama to separate you. Don't allow past mistakes to block the flow of your love.

I remember there were periods of time when Crystal and I were not in a good place in our relationship. We both allowed years of unforgiveness to keep us separated. Time was wasted as I look back at it now, all we needed to do was to FORGIVE, LET IT GO and LOVE AGAIN.

If you are around those who are grieving, allow them to do that. Yes, check on them to make sure they are not falling into depression. Make sure they are sleeping and eating but give them TIME. They may never go back to their NORM, but God will work on them to create a new NORM that will guide them through this season in their life.

Grieving with Grace

Grieving is not easy. It's hard. And you may not feel like dealing with the pain of it all. I understand it. Allow yourself time to grieve. There isn't a time limit on grieving so allow yourself the time to do so. The process is not easy and the feelings you may experience should not be pushed aside or avoided. Feel the feelings. Cry, if you need to. It's okay. You will be living in a new norm, and it will take time to adjust and even accept it. Identify someone or some people that you can talk with so you don't get overwhelmed with managing your feelings and so you don't fall into depression. Take your time.

Transparency Moment – January 28, 2019
Help Me…Help them.

After ministering the word yesterday at our annual women's conference, I was leaving out the sanctuary to change out of my robe. The service continued and everyone was asked to hug someone in the church. I began to hug people as I was leaving out of the sanctuary. The last person I hugged was my granddaughter, Jasmine. At some point, I was about to let her go, but I noticed she wouldn't let me go. I continued to hug her, and she began to cry and all I could say was, "I love you, Jasmine. I've always loved you and we'll get through this together."

As I walked back to the office to change, my heart felt heavy. All I could say was, "God, help me. God help me to help her. Help me to be a strength for someone else."

It Taught Me

I share this because you never know who needs your smile, your hug, your kind words, and your listening ear. You never know who needs your strength that you received from God to help them be strong again. You never know the impact and/or difference that you can make on somebody else's life.

Grieving with Grace

Sometimes while you're going through the grieving process you may not feel strong or even feel like you can help anyone. Afterall, you're grieving. Presently, you need support from others yourself. However, sometimes you will experience an inner strength that will push you beyond your pain and cause you to be a support to someone else suffering loss. I've experienced this myself several times throughout my grieving process.

Somehow God will give you the strength that you need at the exact time you need it. I'm not sure where you are in your grieving process but know that strength is coming and is available for you to help you push through your pain. God's strength is made perfect in your weakness (2 Corinthians 12:9). Lean on Him. He's strong enough and He can handle the weight of your lean.

Transparency Moment – January 31, 2019
God's Strength

I'm amazed at God's strength during the time of weakness. He is powerful and wants us to be STRONG. I'm reminded of a song my husband wrote: Can you smile in the midst of the rain? We think we can't because the tough times are so hard. Believe me when I say, losing a loved one is hard, but I must say that in the midst, God is pouring His strength upon me. Remembering the good times about your loved one can form a smile on your face amid your grieving.

During the grieving process, I found myself drawing from the strength of God. So many times, I was so sad about losing my daughter so quickly that I felt weak and hopeless, but I relinquished my weakness to embody His strength. Please take a moment to read II Corinthians 12:9 it is so true! God's strength is made perfect in our weakness.

<u>It Taught Me</u>

Whether it's grieving or whatever you may be going through, God wants you to make it through. By leaning on the strength of God, HIS WORD and through prayer, you can keep going. God still has great things in store for your life and He is willing to empower you with HIS strength to keep going. Don't ever stop! You must keep going…even your loved one would want you to do so. Tap into God's strength and keep going.

Grieving with Grace

During your grieving process, you may not feel strong at all and that's okay. You are not obligated to walk in strength. As a matter of fact, being strong is difficult during the grieving process. However, what I am emphasizing is for you to lean on God for strength. Pull from Him. He can handle your pull. Lean on those who are supportive of you during this time. Get the support you need to help you through this time and for the many days ahead.

Transparency Moment – February 7, 2019
It Happened So Fast

The other night, Jasmine and I were coming back from the store. I felt the need to share with her about her mom (my daughter), Crystal and the days leading up to her passing. I guess I just needed to talk it out because everything happened so fast. That's actually the first lines of a writing I'm doing on her passing....IT HAPPENED SO FAST.

So, as I was sharing, Jasmine began to ask questions about what happened. As I got out of the car, I was asking Jasmine a question, but she didn't answer me. So, I went around to the other side of the car to find her crying. I immediately grabbed her and said, "I hate that your mother is gone. I hate it, but we must keep going. We must keep going. We have so much that we still need to do." She wiped her tears, and I wiped mine and we both agreed that it's going to take us time to get through this.

It Taught Me

It happened so fast. One minute we were laughing, arguing, separating, reconnecting and then she was gone! If I could turn back the hands of time, I would handle things differently, but I know I can't do that. One thing I've learned: You know what people say, "Here today and gone tomorrow." Take it seriously. Love your family and spend time with them. Time is valuable and spending time with those you love is so important. Make the time. Forgive. Let stuff go.

Time moves fast. Many of us have the notion that we have time to do this and time to do that. However, as you live your life you can attest that you look back and realize time has flown by since the last time you _____ or since the last time you saw _____ or the last time you did _____. It goes to show you that time moves quickly and should be valued.

ENCOURAGING THOUGHT: When this transparency moment was written I felt this about the year for encouragement (you can take it for now): I believe this is a year that things we desired to happen for us will be released. You put the time in and now it's time to see a manifestation. You will find yourself saying, "It happened so fast." "God did it just that quick."

You must keep going. There is so much you STILL need to do. Even though rough times come (they come to all of us), you can't get stuck in the rough time, the sad time, the breakup, the disappointments, the let downs, the losses; you must keep going. Because in your moving forward, something far greater awaits you.

Grieving with Grace

Losing your loved one may have seemed as though it happened so fast. From the time you lose a loved one, plan/organize a funeral, have the funeral and then see their remains lowered in the grave or remains placed in an urn....it feels like you've been in a whirlwind. So many emotions surround you and it's hard to brace yourself. It happened so fast.... It may take time to recover depending on who you lost and your connection with them. Give yourself space to process your feelings and emotions at your own pace.

Transparency Moment – February 22, 2019
The New Norm

I must admit yesterday was a little rough. Still trying to process that Crystal is no longer here. I know life is going on and I'm moving accordingly, but it all seems like a blur. Inwardly, I'm trying to get back to the norm only to realize that the old norm doesn't exist anymore. The new norm has emerged. Things are different, adjustments must be made, healing must manifest completely, tears have to be shed, reflections of good times must be pondered and even the times when things were not right between us must be evaluated. I'm learning some things through this process. Writing about it helps.

<u>It Taught Me</u>

The old norm is gone. Moving on is a process and it is also a necessity. You can't get stuck (which I'm working on). When things take place in your life that are disappointing, YOU CAN'T SIT IN THE DISAPPOINTMENT. You can't stay there. You must keep moving. Allow God to heal you and move on. You can't go back to the old nor can you change it...you must walk in the new norm---the new man. Let go of the past and move forward with grace. Great things are right in front of you.

The Merriam-Webster dictionary's definition of Stuck - firmly positioned in place and difficult to dislodge. This is the tactic of the enemy for many of us to get stuck in our situation, our hurt, our disappointments etc. - because if the enemy can get us to remain there (STUCK), he knows we'll never fulfill God's plan. Time to get UNSTUCK (talking to me too) ...time to move on, time to show up, time to walk in your divine purpose, it's time to fulfill your dream.... IT'S TIME!

Grieving with Grace

When grieving, you don't necessarily want to accept it, much less move beyond the old way of living and doing things in a new way. In your mind you want everything to go back to the way it was...back to your loved one being alive so you can be with them, love them, fix some things and maybe even start fresh, but when reality sinks in you realize a new norm have begun. Take your time. You're walking in new territory and at times it may be hard to keep going, but you will get through it.

After losing someone you may indeed have feelings of being stuck. It feels as though you're at a standstill. The world is moving around you, but you feel stuck in the time zone of your loss. It's okay. It's part of the process and as time moves forward you will be able to flow back into your life gradually. Please give yourself some grace because you've never gone through anything like this before (or maybe you have….it still doesn't make it easy). Walk through it and don't rush to get past your grieving time. Take the time to process your feelings and emotions at your own pace.

Transparency Moment – February 22, 2019
Things are Birthed out of Pain

I was sitting here thinking.... Lord, you got to get me through this. I've been having these feelings of just being stuck, feelings of being on pause. I know it has a lot to do with my daughter's passing, but I can feel my spirit tugging at me to get up and do what God has placed inside of me. Don't let time pass you by. I must get past this. I just said, "Lord, I want to be a vessel of honor. I want to bring you glory. How can I do it while I'm feeling this pain?" Then the thought dropped in my spirit...things are birthed out of pain...

It Taught Me

I immediately thought about when a woman gives birth to a child. The pain is at times unbearable!!! It starts off slowly and then it speeds up so fast that you just want it to end, but you can't rush through the pain. You must wait until that baby is ready to be released from your womb. In the midst, you endure it and you push when it's time to push because that baby has to come out of you. The baby (your dream, goals, ministry, business...) must come out of YOU. You must do this!!! You've been anointed and destined to do some great things.

The pain is real.... but you must endure it, push past it and birth what God has placed in you. Things are born out of pain. The anointing upon your life is still there. The dreams you had when you were young are still in your spirit...push past the pain. The Holy Spirit is the midwife screaming out.... PUSH!!! You can do this. You can get through this. Something good is coming out of this.

Grieving with Grace

Many purposes are birthed out of pain. You may be thinking that this grieving process is the hardest thing you've ever encountered. The pain and sadness of it all makes you want to give up, but you can't. There are some very phenomenal people in this world who have had painful situations and suffered loss, but they didn't allow it to keep them down forever. Someday you will be able to comfort another through their loss. I will tell you that the intensity of the feelings of sadness will subside in time. Believe me, you will. I'm a witness.

Transparency Moment – February 25, 2019
Standstill

I was in my kitchen washing dishes and I began to ask God what was going on with me. I began to say, "God, I feel like I'm at a standstill." "What is happening?" So, I took the time to look at the word in the Merriam-Webster dictionary. Standstill: a state characterized by absence of motion or of progress.

I pondered this for a couple of days. Standstill...hmmm. I know some progress is being made, but it's slow. It still feels like a standstill. So then, I began to think about God's Word. I remembered in Exodus 14:13 where Moses told the children of Israel not to fear, but to stand still and SEE the salvation of the Lord. The Holy Spirit ministered to me.... Stephanie, you need to SEE! You can't get stuck by what is going on around you. You must begin to SEE beyond the standstill. Beyond the standstill is the breakthrough, beyond the standstill is what you dreamed of, what you've been praying for, what you've been destined for. You need to SEE. I began to pray.... LORD, HELP ME TO SEE!

It Taught Me

2 Kings 6:15-17 - Elisha prayed that his servant's eyes be opened. "I pray thee, open his eyes, that he may see." And the servant's eyes were open. When we allow our circumstances to paralyze us, we need God to open our eyes so we can SEE. See beyond what's happening (I got to do this as well) - see what you want to manifest in your life.

Then I thought about Psalm 27:13.... David was about to faint unless he believed to SEE....

Open up your spiritual eyes and SEE.....don't get stuck in the standstill because there is so many great things that you're destined for. LORD, HELP ME TO SEE!

Grieving with Grace

The feelings of being at a standstill came because of losing my daughter to cancer. I felt so stuck and at times I still do. Going through the motions but not fully present with reality. I was at a standstill. Maybe you feel this way too. Maybe losing the one you loved so dearly has caused your life, as you know it now, to be at a standstill. Take a moment to breathe. Take a moment to remember what made you smile. What was your dream? What was your vision before the loss? See that...again. Ask God to help you to see. Beyond the standstill there is so much more to experience in your life. Be willing to take the step beyond the standstill, beyond the anger and sadness. There is still so much more for your life ahead of you.

Transparency Moment – February 26, 2019
Closure

The word closure is defined as this in the Merriam-Webster Dictionary....Closure: an often comforting or satisfying sense of finality. This was the day I had enough courage to call the doctor's office just to find out what really happened to my daughter, Crystal. I've been wanting to make this call to the doctor for weeks, but I just couldn't bring myself to do it. Don't get me wrong, I'm not losing it. I already know what happened, but I just needed some closure to bring a resolve to some of the thoughts that have been racing through my mind. It was those things the doctor initially mentioned in the treatment process that continued to play back in my head. So, I had to hear from him to bring closure to the questions and concerns that I'd been pondering for some time. As I think about it.... tears are forming in my eyes. This is hard, but God is truly comforting me in the midst. I'm okay.... I just have to bring closure.

<u>It Taught Me</u>

Bringing closure to some things really helps with the healing process. I may not understand everything, but I must bring closure to my questions. Sometimes we can't fully move forward until we have brought some closure to some things. There may be some relationships, feelings of unforgiveness, bitterness, or some emotional hurt and pains that you really need to resolve. There may even be some old ways (sins) that you still feel the need to gravitate to that you need to completely stop. Closing some doors may be necessary to bring something greater into your life. Bring closure to the things that don't mean you well. Close those doors so you can experience something far greater.... PEACE OF MIND.

Even though I've got to bring closure to these unanswered questions, it doesn't mean I'll forget about my daughter (that I can never do), but at least those things can be settled to aid me through this process. As one person put it, "I'm progressing through the process." Yes, bringing closure is a sign of progress that I know that I needed to do to move forward.

What are the things that you need to bring closure to? Closing it may not be as difficult as you think. Closing "it" may open something so much greater than you could ever imagine. What will you bring closure to today?

Grieving with Grace

There are some things that you can do to bring closure when it comes to grieving the loss of your loved one. Journaling is a way to help you process the loss. Take the time to write a letter to your loved one and share with them some things that you wanted them to know. You can write your thoughts and feelings in your journal about what you need to bring closure to. Oftentimes, therapists will use the empty chair technique to help people process trauma by imagining the person you want to bring closure to in an empty chair. Begin to say what you need to say to the empty chair. I've done this after my father passed away. There were things I still needed to tell him to bring some peace about his passing. Sometimes when processing your loss, you may consider seeing a therapist. Counseling will help you to process your feelings of grief in a safe space. Please don't walk this journey alone. Talk with someone to help you through it.

Transparency Moment – March 4, 2019
Keep Going Don't Stop

I had an opportunity to speak at a Women's Conference on Saturday, March 2, 2019. It was truly a blessing. The theme was: "Keep Going, Don't Stop." At the time when I received the invite from Denetra Washington, it was during the time of the passing of my daughter. I really felt like God was talking to me personally. I got to keep going....don't stop. Well, on my way to the speaking engagement, I happened to pass by the cemetery. As I drove past it.... I thought about my daughter. I hadn't been to the site since her homegoing service. Then I realized that it was 3 months to the day that she had passed. So, I thought to myself, I will drive by there on the way back from speaking.

As I was ministering the word from I Samuel 16:1, I realized that God was speaking to me as he was speaking to those women. You got to keep moving...don't stop. God had to address the Prophet Samuel about his length of time of mourning over King Saul and his disobedience. God had already moved on and was wondering why Samuel was stuck. God immediately said, fill thine horne with oil and go! In other words, get up from there Samuel and walk in your divine assignment. God has something He wants you to do, and you can't let nothing, not one thing, not a divorce, not a betrayal, not disappointments, not a broken relationship, not even a death of a loved one or of a child to keep you from YOUR assignment. You must keep going...don't stop. I repeat YOU MUST KEEP GOING....DON'T STOP. One of things that I told those ladies that if the devil thought because I loss my daughter, that I was going to give up on God....he was sadly mistaken. I can't turn my back on the One who is my source of strength.

Well, after I sat down from speaking, the tears were coming, and I wanted to just cry hysterically because I didn't realize how deep this hit me. Under the anointing you can speak boldly, but when you sit down.... you feel the emotions. I was so glad that one of the speakers took her hand and rubbed my back. Just a simple rub on the back calmed me down. Thank God. You never know what a touch will do for someone.

Afterwards, I went by the cemetery and at first, I couldn't find her place, but when I did.......well, you know...the tears flowed. I still couldn't believe that she was not here anymore. I wept and I asked God to help me and to give me the strength to keep going. Don't stop. I won't forget her, but I MUST KEEP GOING.

It Taught Me

Never give up on you. You must believe in yourself and advocate for yourself. Keep going, don't stop. Whatever hardship you may face in life, pick up the pieces and keep going. Whatever remains give it to God and allow Him to help you through. Just beyond your next steps is the breakthrough you've been waiting for. Take the leap, push forward, keep going.

Grieving with Grace

I know it feels like a part of you has stopped. At times it may be difficult to keep going after loss, but that is truly what you must do. You must keep going…don't stop. You are alive, you are still here, and you have a purpose to fulfill. Your loved one would want you to keep living. This new norm can be very hard initially, but you will get through it. The key is to not get stuck in sadness or gravitate to depression, but to keep going. Don't stop.

Transparency Moment – March 8, 2019
Mother/Daughter Connection

Yesterday, I was going to the store to pick out a dress for my birthday dinner (EXCITED!!!). As I was getting out of the car, I saw someone I hadn't seen in a long time. She saw me and came to greet me with a hug. We said our hellos and then I noticed she was pregnant. I was happy to see that she was. She mentioned that it was a girl and that she was looking forward to the mother/daughter times. I mentioned to her about how much fun it's going to be.

As I looked at her and heard her say that I couldn't help but think about my daughter, Crystal. I had to catch myself because I realized that she and I wouldn't have any mother/daughter experiences again. I just wanted to call Crystal yesterday just to see how she was, but I realized I knew I couldn't. God got her....and I'm truly happy about her making it to Heaven.

I've got to share this: Crystal and I had some very good times when we did (we had good laughs), but then there were times when things were not right at all. When things were not right, it kept us from having those mother/daughter experiences. I'm glad that we were able to resolve some things prior to her death. For that I am thankful. But I often regret that we didn't resolve the issues sooner.

It Taught Me

I say this because if you have a daughter or even a son that is alive and things are not right between the two of you.....FIX IT. Do whatever you have to do (FORGIVE, SWALLOW PRIDE, LOVE AGAIN, TRUST AGAIN....) to make things right with your children. This goes for children as well. Make things right with your parents. Do it! Don't let anger, old mistakes or pride block you from the relationship you are supposed to have with your parents. God is good. I'm grateful for being able to share the times that we did. She will always be my "Pookie."

Spend time with those you love. Do it. No excuses, make the time. It's important and it's something everyone involved will always remember.

Grieving with Grace

Memories of your loved one will always be with you. At times when you are feeling sad, or missing them, take a moment to remember the good memories you shared. Reflect on those memories and write about how they made you feel whenever you feel the desire to do so. If there is someone that you need to reconcile with that is connected to the one you lost, do that too. Make peace with those that you need to.

Transparency Moment – March 19, 2019
Prayer

During revival last week, the guest speaker prayed for me concerning my daughter. What he shared with me was encouraging. For years my daughter was in and out of church. Through those years our relationship was on and off. At times the enemy would use her to fight against me because of the anger she felt towards me. The speaker mentioned that a "spirit" would come upon her and cause her to be this way. I made a choice several years ago and ever since that time she held it against me. She would constantly throw it up in my face whenever she got upset. Looking back now, I believe I would have handled things differently. I understand now that all she wanted was my love. She wanted things to be like they were...the close connection that we once had. At the time I couldn't see that because I thought she hated me. This troubled me for years until one day I decided that I was not going to continue to beat myself up because of it; nor would I allow anyone else to. I often wondered would we ever reconcile; would we ever be as close again. At the onset of her illness, we were able to reconcile and make peace with one another. For that I am grateful. I love my daughter and I miss her dearly. I sat down with Jasmine last night and tried to ask her what she felt about me and her mom. We talked about anger, holding grudges, forgiveness, and love. I mentioned that I hated that we wasted so much time not letting old stuff go. Jasmine and I talked about the good laughs and talks the three of us had. I guess she and I are helping each other to heal through this.

But then the Man of God told me that my prayers for my daughter spared her at the last minute so that she would go to Heaven. My daughter is in Heaven. For that I am grateful. This reinforced to me the power of prayer and that prayer still works.

It Taught Me
It doesn't matter what may be happening around you, prayer can change everything. Don't underestimate the power of prayer. You may say, but I prayed for my loved one to live and they didn't. I understand. I felt that way at some point during my grieving process too. Not exactly sure why that happens sometimes but focus on the many other prayers that God did answer. Focus on that and keep praying.

Forgive. Let those old hurts go. Allow God to heal. Stop focusing on the issue; focus on what you can do to resolve the issue. So many times, when there are disagreements and fallouts with family, they often focus on what they did and the pain they caused, but seldom do they try to find a solution or come to an agreement.

Next time, look for ways to resolve it, and not add more pain to it.

Grieving with Grace

During the grieving process, you will need to spend time in prayer. You might even be thinking that you prayed before the loss and your loved one still died. As I said, I'm not sure of why that happens, but I do know that prayer will help you release any pain and sadness you may feel. Cast your cares upon the Lord because He cares for you. He cares enough to carry the burden and give you the strength you need to get you through this time of grieving and beyond. Keep praying there is still so much to cover for you and for those who remain.

Transparency Moment – April 1, 2019
A Better Place

How can you really tell a 15-year-old that her mother is in a better place when in her eyes a better place is having her mom with her? Yesterday was a bit challenging for my granddaughter, Jasmine. Last night when I got in, I asked Jasmine about her weekend away on her ROTC trip. She seemed tired, but a little out of it. I could tell something just wasn't right. I went upstairs in my bedroom and got into bed, but I felt a bit restless. I believe it was the Holy Spirit that told me to go check on Jasmine again. When I did, she started crying......oh my. All I could do was grab her and rub her back and tell her to let it out. I whispered a prayer for her and just sat there for a while. I tried to reassure her that the pain of her loss would one day ease up (I know because I know what it feels like to lose a mother). It's hard to share that with a 15-year-old who happened to be so close to her mom. I told her that her mother will never be forgotten by her or anyone else she was connected to, but the pain of her loss will eventually lift in time. I'm asking God to give me strength, but I also need God to give strength and comfort to Jasmine.

It Taught Me

The Holy Spirit is powerful. He will guide you. Sometimes the Holy Spirit will share with you when to do something, say something or even give something to help another. We never know when someone will need our help, support, comfort or even a rub on the back. When you love someone, you cover them through their pain until they can stand on their own. Who is the Holy Spirit leading you to be a blessing to or to be a support to them? Follow the leading of the Holy Spirit. Ask Him who you may need to comfort.

Grieving with Grace

We often hear people say that "they are in a better place." I know that sounds cliché and I'm not totally sure it's comforting in every situation. When you hear that expression, you may feel like the better place is with you and with your family. However, if your loved one was in pain, it's good to know that they no longer are enduring the pain. At times, it's hard to accept that they are gone. It will take time to accept it. In the days moving forward allow God to comfort you through your time of grief.

They are in a better place. Have you ever heard someone say this? How did it make you feel? Were there any other things that people said to you that you didn't feel fitting during your grieving? Reflect and journal your thoughts.

Transparency Moment – April 12, 2019
Out of My Hands

There is not a day that goes by that I don't think about my daughter in some capacity. I was asked to review the days I was out for work for her passing, and it brought some sadness. I looked back over my calendar and saw where I marked on Sunday, December 2, 2018, that Crystal went to go be with God. It's hard for that to sink in sometimes, but I recognize that this is reality and the new norm. I can remember the last visit on Saturday, November 17, 2018, that I had with Crystal where she was able to communicate. It was a good visit and I really felt she was going to be okay. She was so excited to see me, and I was so excited to see her. Little did I know that it would be the last time that I would really be able to communicate with her. This brings some sadness, but I must remember that she is out of pain. I had hoped that God would have healed her on this side of Heaven, but knowing she made it into Heaven is my consolation.

Shortly after her death, I must admit, I wondered if I had prayed enough, had I spoken positive affirmations about her healing enough? Did I fail her in not praying for her through this? I mean, I know I prayed, but was I supposed to pray harder? I had so many questions, but then I had to come to the realization that there was nothing I could do. It was out of my hands.

It Taught Me

Sometimes we may feel as though things aren't going the way we planned or the way we anticipated. At times we may feel as though we've failed in some way. We did all we could, yet it didn't quite go the way we wanted it to. Listen, when we yield our plan to the plan of God - He will direct us. Sometimes it's not supposed to go the way you planned because God has another agenda. Sometimes we must sit down, be still and hear God. He will speak.

As I said with Crystal, IT WAS OUT OF MY HANDS. Sometimes things are out of our hands, which means you can't control it. When things are out of our hands, that means we must totally trust God for everything. Out of your hands is a position of surrendering. What will you release out of your hands into the hands of God today?

Grieving with Grace

There may have been times that you wished you could turn the hands of time and do something different to keep your loved one alive. Oftentimes, questions may play back in your mind of how you could have handled things differently. Maybe you had thoughts of wishing you spent more time with them, talked with them more or even forgave them. However, you realize sooner than later that things are out of your hands. Know that whatever you were supposed to do for your loved one, you did to the best of your ability at that time. Rest in knowing that.

Transparency Moment – April 23, 2019
Counseling

Last month I'd been thinking about some things concerning my daughter's loss and our relationship. Some things I was still wrestling with concerning the past. The words exchanged through the years began to resurface as well as the feelings that went along with it. I knew I could cast it over to the Lord, but I still needed someone to hear my truth. So, I made an appointment with my counselor (yes, I have one). Since I've been studying in the field of counseling, it's advised that we get counseling as well to understand the process that our future clients would experience. They also suggested we get counseling to address any unresolved issues that we may be facing so that it doesn't trickle down into our counseling with others. I'm an advocate for counseling. I've had one for years and I'm not ashamed of it because it has helped me tremendously. I know losing a loved one can be traumatic and the process of grieving is a difficult process. I wouldn't in a million years try to walk this path alone. For those of you who say, "I got Jesus and that's all I need." - God bless you. I admire your strength. However, don't knock those who seek counsel. There are some people who really need to sit down with someone to process the things they've experienced. A lot of times the reason some people are catching hell now is because they haven't addressed some of the things they so desperately try to hide from the past.

The scriptures say: Where no counsel is, the people fall: but in the multitude of counsellors there is safety. (Proverbs 11:14). Counseling brings balance and safety.

It Taught Me

So, I sat with the counselor and shared my truth about my daughter and all that was still unsettled in my heart. I began to express the choices I made and why I made them. I realized that through the session I made choices based on what I knew THEN to be the right thing to do. I did the best I could, and I've got to accept that for what it is. I also realized that had I known then what I know NOW....I would have handled things differently. However, the key is I can't beat myself up for how things went. Also, the people in your life that hold things against you or never want to forgive you, but instead want to hold you hostage because of your past.... RELEASE THEM. If they aren't going to forgive you, then don't waste your life trying to convince them to do so. It's not worth it. Forgive yourself and move on.

Grieving with Grace

I'm truly an advocate for counseling. I can't emphasize enough that it is so important not to walk this journey of grieving alone. Talking with a therapist helps you to process the trauma that you are experiencing from the loss of your loved one. You need a safe space to heal. Sometimes others around you may not understand your pain and may even try to convince you that you need to move on and move past it all at their pace. But that it so far fetched from your reality. Talking with a professional counselor gives you an opportunity to express your feelings in a non-bias setting and will give you the time you need to process it all without being rushed to get over it. Counseling will help provide the tools you need to help you cope. I am also a firm believer that it's so important to talk with God. Talking to God is what I did. I leaned on God's big shoulders filled with strength to help me through. Along with God, I believe it's good to talk about your feelings and sharing it with a counselor is an added benefit. Seek out some counseling to walk you through this grieving process. Don't do it alone.

Transparency Moment – May 7, 2019
Three Years turn to Thirty Days

I was thinking back on a conversation that Crystal and I had after she spoke with her doctor in Charleston. She had been in the hospital for close to two weeks and at that point we were looking for answers to combat this cancer. Her doctor shared with her another option of fighting cancer because at that point her body had totally rejected the chemo they were using. I still have mixed emotions about the entire process. So, when the doctor told her about the new option, she and I got excited. Thinking about it now seemed so crazy. He shared with her that the new option would give her more time to live, but it was only for 3 years. We got excited about it because it was beyond what they originally told her, which was 1 year to live.

You know, after my daughter heard about her 1 year to live diagnosis, she wasn't even paying them any attention about it because she was believing that God was going to turn it around for her. Looking back, I remember us getting excited about those 3 years to live.... wow! She wanted more time to live and more time to be with her children. However, the new option only lasted 30 days and after those days she was gone. As I've shared before, it happened so fast. I still wonder sometimes what happened. I mean the new medication dosage only worked for 30 days. After bringing closure with her doctor, I learned that this cancer was extremely aggressive. The thought of her having 3 years to live seemed like the best news we had heard since her first diagnosis.

It Taught Me

I gather from this that it's not a matter of how much time you have, but more so what you do with the time you have. LIVE AND ENJOY YOUR LIFE! Sometimes we complain about some of the strangest things, we allow certain circumstances to move us so much and take us off track, we argue and don't forgive the ones we love.

Don't waste your life being connected to individuals that bring you down. Your life is too valuable to allow negativity of others to reduce your level of joy in your life. Take vacations and spend time with family. Be thankful for what you have. Be thankful for who is in your life right now. Be thankful that you have the breath of life.

Grieving with Grace

Maybe during your experience of losing your loved one, you had a glimmer of hope for their healing or recovery only to find out it was too late, and they were gone. I know it's very hard to accept this. You may find yourself going back and forth with the stages of grief, but once you get to the point of acceptance, I hope you will be able to reminisce about the good memories of the one you love. As time moves forward, I hope you have the strength to create new memories with those who remain.

Transparency Moment – May 10, 2019
1:23 a.m.

When I read over my daughter's death certificate (oh my) for the 3rd time, I noticed something I hadn't really paid attention to when I first glanced at it. Initially, I couldn't believe I was holding the death certificate of my daughter who had only been 36 years old.... wow! So, I really didn't look at it closely. However, at the third time, I noticed the time of her death. It read 0123....she passed at 01:23 a.m. I remember being restless that night because I knew I was going to get the call from the Hospice nurse at any time. When she called, I answered and said, "This is the call...isn't it?" She replied, "Yes, I'm so sorry...." I went to the hospital shortly after the call to see her body in the bed lifeless. A memory I will never forget because I couldn't believe someone with so much LIFE was gone. Boy, that was tough. She went to be with God. I remember writing this on the calendar on December 2, 2018, Crystal went to be with God.

It Taught Me
The thought came to me again about the timing of her death....1:23. I gleaned a nugget from that information. There is an order, sequence, process for how things should be done. There are things that we want to do, accomplish, and pursue (dreams, goals, business ventures, ministry, use of creative ability), but we must

keep in mind that there is an order, a sequence, a process of things to happen, a specific timing for it all and even time for things to be completed. We can't jump ahead of the timing of God. We can't rush it or try to bypass every step and piece of the puzzle. Things must be done in order. We must go through the process to achieve whatever we want in life. If we want it to be right, we must follow the order - the process. Even in my time of grieving I can't rush it. I can't jump over it hoping it will go away. I can't pack it down or push the emotions down just so I can put a smile on my face. I've got to go through the process. When we rush the order or the process, we may miss a vital lesson, we may miss a point of healing, deliverance, or breakthrough. Don't let people rush you through your process. Learn what you need to learn and do it right.

There is an order, a structure, a sequence of time that we must follow. If we stay connected to God and receive the instructions and follow them EXACTLY, we'll find that doing so will create a greater outcome.

I miss my daughter.... last night especially. I really wanted to talk and share a good laugh. However, I know there was a process that she had to experience as well. She made it to Glory!

Grieving with Grace

Grieving is a process that should not be rushed but allowed to run its course at your pace. Take your time to heal from your loss. Don't allow others to rush you. Everyone grieves differently, so don't compare your process to someone else's. The only thing to consider is to not get stuck in the process. Don't get stuck in your pain. It is a process and it's meant to keep moving. You will get through this. Really. You will.

Transparency Moment – May 13, 2019
First Mother's Day

I thought this Mother's Day was going to be tough for Jasmine, but I got to give it to her --- she was strong. I had an opportunity to speak at a church for their Mother's Day message and she came along with me. As the church members were giving accolades to their mothers, I couldn't help but glance at her from time to time from the pulpit. She was good. After I preached, she said I did great! Then later that day once I finally got home, she said, "Mama, I got something for you." And she gave me a 3-piece set of one of my favorite smell goods from Bath and Body Works. I'm thanking God for her. It's tough I know for her and for me, but I hope in the midst of it all she sees a light in me that will help her through her journey.

It Taught Me

I've got to take heed to the message I ministered yesterday, "I See It in You." 2 Timothy 1:3-5 - Paul recognized the unfeigned faith in Timothy, but you can't ignore the fact that Timothy possessed that unfeigned faith because Lois (his grandmother) taught it to Eunice (his mother) and Eunice taught it to Timothy. Our children/grandchildren should see a light, hope, love, forgiveness in us so that they will live it and pass it down to their children. What do your children see in you? What are you passing on to the next generation?

Grieving with Grace

When grieving you must remember that you are not the only one hurting through the loss. There are other family members that are impacted just as much as you are. Sometimes your lost loved one has children, grandchildren, nieces, nephews, cousins, parents etc. that need encouragement during the time of loss also. Yes, you need to be comforted, but sometimes reaching out to others in the family will help both of you. Together you can help one another to get through all of this. It's okay to lean on one another from time to time. Work together to bring comfort to one another during this time.

What did you learn from them? As I shared about the scripture in 2 Timothy 1:3-5, it reveals that Timothy had this unfeigned faith that was noticeable. He learned from his mother and grandmother. Was there something that your loved one taught you? Feel free to share it here or in your journal.

Transparency Moment – May 21, 2019
Mother/Daughter Tea

I must admit I was a little nervous about attending the Mother/Daughter Tea Social that I was sponsoring for the girls mentoring program. I wondered would I be able to get through the event knowing that my daughter would not be attending. I even mentioned it to my granddaughter hoping that she would come with me to somewhat ease my anxiety. When I mentioned it to her, she and I both paused and was like.... oh boy! Through the planning, I kept thinking if I can just get through this, I'll be alright. I was wondering was I going to cry through the presentations and activities or what. Anyway, it turned out that the day of the event, my granddaughter didn't attend (she was asleep in bed). She probably didn't want to be there either, so I didn't push it. I went to the event and the girls assisted me with decorating and getting things prepared. At the event, the mothers were saying so many kind things about their daughters and to hear even the beautiful words shared by the daughters to their mothers was amazing.

I thought to myself, I must continue to do this because the bond between a mother and daughter is so valuable. It's so important to rebuild and heal the mother and daughter relationship. I wish I could have done things differently with my own daughter, but as I'm writing this, I realize I have another opportunity and that is with my granddaughter and with the many other spiritual daughters that I will connect with. I must say I am grateful to God for giving me the strength to get through the Mother/Daughter tea. I didn't cry, but I enjoyed being there for the experience.

It Taught Me

Sometimes we think we can't handle something, but when we draw from the strength of God, He will bring us through. That's not to say it won't be tough (because it was for me), but God will carry you through if you lean and trust in Him.

I also realized that this event was for the girls and their mothers, and it really wasn't about me. It was about them. Sometimes we get caught up in making it about us, when really the things you do or say are not just for you, but they influence and impact others. Sometimes we must step away from our concerns to be there for another. I'm glad I was there. I'm glad I experienced it and I'm glad those that attended were blessed.

Grieving with Grace

As I said, being at this event was tough for me, but I pressed through to be present. Sometimes you will have to push through your pain to be present for those that may need you. I understand that while you are grieving you may not feel like or even be up to being there for someone else. Keep in mind that you may have to support someone else in the family that is grieving the loss as well. Pushing through together to support each other may be needed. Sometimes being supportive of them will also help you get through this time as well.

Transparency Moment – May 28, 2019
Triggers

A trigger is something that sets off a memory or flashback transporting the person back to the event of her/his original trauma. Triggers are very personal. People, places and different things have the potential to trigger individuals differently. The survivor may begin to avoid situations and stimuli that she/he thinks triggered the flashback.

Sometimes we may not understand why people do what they do or say what they say. Sometimes events, words, music, people, aromas can trigger a person to remember an event or a life experience.

I love going to church so please don't take this the wrong way when I write this. Sundays at times are difficult for me because it was Sunday, December 2, 2018, that my daughter, Crystal passed away to be with the Lord at 1:23 a.m. This past Sunday we had an amazing service at church but driving to church I had a trigger moment. My mind played a memory tape of the morning Crystal died. I said to my husband, after receiving the call from the Hospice nurse, "Crystal died." I remember him giving me a hug and saying, "Wow, you're so strong." My only response was, "I'm going to the hospital to see her." So, I went there for only a few moments to view her body. That same day, I went to church that morning to tell the members that Crystal had died that morning. It was the hardest announcement I ever had to make.

So, this Sunday, I had a trigger after the message was preached by one of the ministers in my church. I don't know if my husband even knew this, but he grabbed my hand during the worship, and we continued to worship God. However, during that moment I cried from a deep place of hurt. It's a hurt I can't even explain in words, but it's deep. A place that only God can heal and mend. Don't worry.... I'm okay. I must go through the process and not rush it. I began to ask God to help me. Somehow, he happened to use my husband's hand to give me added strength.

It Taught Me

So, I say this again, sometimes we don't understand totally why people do what they do, say what they say or act the way they do around certain circumstances. It could very well be that something has triggered them to react and respond the way that they did.

Be mindful of the things that trigger you. Examine your reaction to those triggers and ask God to help you cope when those feelings arise.

As I mentioned, my husband held my hand. It gave me added strength. You never know when someone will just need your hand for strength. You never know when someone will need your smile or your encouraging words just to give them that extra push of hope. As you were comforted, go back and comfort someone that may need it too (2 Corinthians 1:3-4).

Grieving with Grace

It's important to know what your triggers are during this grieving process. Take time to identify them. Make others aware of these triggers so they will know how to comfort you during this time. Don't be afraid or feel like a burden to let someone know that you need them when you feel triggered, sad, or overwhelmed. These feelings are normal during the grieving process. The key is to reach out to someone or others when needed. Don't try to carry this burden alone.

Transparency Moment – June 10, 2019
LIVE

The other day I had this strange dream and in it I was saying I haven't talked to Crystal in a long time and then I was like she hasn't called me either. I started wondering if she was upset with me or something. Then in the dream I realized she wasn't here anymore. I am finding that throughout this process of grieving it will take time to process all the emotions that go along with it. Sometimes you think the person is just at their house and you can go by there, but when reality sinks in, you know you can't. You come to realize that you must move on and keep going.

I had someone recently share with me that Crystal is gone and she's not coming back. I thought to myself, this is true, but I also realized that sometimes people want you to rush your grief process, your healing process, your true deliverance process to accommodate them. The process becomes difficult for them, but you must consider that it's not about them, it's about you being whole in God. Now, don't get me wrong, I'm not saying sit in your grief and roll over into depression, stagnation and hopelessness.... DON'T DO THAT. Allow God to heal you through it and show you what He has in store for your life. It's about you being healed and being restored. It's about you fully overcoming the pain of the loss and being able to smile again…genuinely.

After talking briefly with another mother, who also lost her daughter years ago, she mentioned something to me that hit home. She said, "YOU are not dead! Your daughter is gone, but you are alive." Let that sink in..... YOU ARE ALIVE!

It Taught Me:

You are not dead! You are alive....so LIVE! You cannot get stuck. You must move on. You must fulfill the divine purpose that God has strategically planned for you. God knew people would leave us, He knew relationships would end, He knew we would experience some setbacks, but you are ALIVE!!! Use what God has given you and LIVE!

Grieving with Grace

During the grieving process it will at times seem unreal that your loved one is no longer here. You may even feel at times that they still exist, and you can give them a call or go to their house. You may even think that one day they will come busting through your front door. In your heart and mind, you truly want to believe that, but you must realize they are no longer here. It's important to move towards acceptance so that you can carry on with your life. Living beyond the loss is difficult, but you are here, and you have a purpose. Please live. They would want you to.

Transparency Moment – June 11, 2019
No Place Like Home

I thought about my daughter, Crystal this morning and a thought dropped in my heart, "I want to go home." As soon as I thought about that statement, tears began to come (even now). Now, I'm not talking about "home" with the Lord (no I don't want to die. I have too much I still have to do to the glory of God. I got to do my assignment). I was thinking about New Jersey. Flashbacks of home, flashbacks of the good times, laughs and some of the experiences I encountered there. It's where it all started for me. I just kept feeling; I want to go home. There are many emotions that come into play with that thought. I'm asking God to help me process it.

It Taught Me

There are a few things that come to mind as I ponder that thought about going home. Some places and/or people are very comforting to us. So, at times when we are going through things, our heart and mind tend to long for those places and/or people that bring us comfort. I'm sure there are some places you like to visit just because it's a place that you enjoyed, had a great experience and you felt some form of comfort. There are some people you just like to connect with simply because they make you feel good, they make you feel valuable, they make you laugh, they know how to build you up. So, in essence those things may make you want to go home to how things used to be.

I want to go home. This could also be tugging for purpose. Home is a place where the foundation is laid. Purpose seeds are planted at home. The authentic you formed when you lived at home. Sometimes we find our spirit speaking to us about going back to the place/purpose that God designed just for us. Some of us can remember some of the good things we used to do or accomplished that brought God glory and inwardly our spirit yearns (cries out) to be at that place again and higher. Do you want to go back to where God first called you? The assignment began there. Take a moment to reflect on when He first called you or drew you to His love.

Sometimes we can't go home. Sometimes it's best not to go back home. Sometimes home exemplifies a comfort zone. A place where we can hide and never come out of. Sometimes God springs us out of home to take us to a greater place to do greater things. Ask Abraham. Many of us must come out of our comfort zone. We must allow God to stretch us and move forward into His plan.

Grieving with Grace

Sometimes while you are grieving you may have those feelings of wanting things to be the same again. You want your loved one back with you. You want another chance to spend time with them, talk with them or even reconcile with them. You want them to be home. You want home to be like it was with them in it. I know it can be difficult to move forward into the new norm. It's okay to reminisce, but there is a new journey ahead of you and God will give you strength along the way.

Transparency Moment – June 13, 2019
Don't Get Stuck in the Pain

"Don't get stuck in the pain." Wow. This is a sentence I shared with another mother who recently lost her child. As I looked over the sentence, the words jumped out at me. "Stephanie McKenny don't get stuck in the pain." Never would I have ever imagined that I would be sending these words to another mother because I could truly relate. Wow. I know it's important to encourage others through trying times, but having to do it from the perspective of enduring the same experience is challenging. I must admit, the last two days have been extremely tough for me - being very sensitive and crying at the drop of a hat. I miss my daughter.... period. Outwardly, I tried so hard to smile, but inwardly the pain was excruciating as if I was in labor. I had to reach out to someone to really pray me through. As they prayed for me, I just cried from a place so deep as if I was travailing and giving birth. Yet during the prayer, God was letting me know that there will be a purposed fulfilled out of this pain. Today, is a better day and I had the strength to type.... don't get stuck in the pain for someone else in pain.

It Taught Me

Whatever you may be experiencing in life seems unbearable, so discouraging, so painful, I would encourage you not to get stuck in the pain of the grief. Focusing on the things that are not right or the things/people missing in our lives only stagnates our progress. You can't stay there. You can't prosper there. It's so important to push past your pain. You must get through this because so many lives are looking for a way to make it and they glean hope from your progress. You can do it. You really can.

I had to reach out. I even shared with the person, I'm not ashamed I NEED PRAYER. Don't ever be afraid or ashamed to get the help you need. Reaching out for help is not a sign of weakness. It is a sign of strength because you have come to the realization that you can't do this by yourself. You just need support right now. Businesspeople do it all the time. When they recognize that the company needs assistance to make it better, they reach out. Reaching out makes you better! Stop trying to hold it all in and pretend you got it all together. It's better to reach out now than explode later!!! The enemy wants God's people to be depressed and suffer in silence. He takes advantage of our pride and feelings of shame because he knows we will remain hidden. Enough of that, reach out and get help.

I'm better today because I reached out and I'm not going to allow myself to get stuck in pain. Hoped this helped you. Blessings.

Grieving with Grace

As you walk through this grieving process, it's so important to get support from others that love you. Doing this alone can cause you to get stuck in the sadness of it all. During the grieving process your emotions are all over the place. The pain of the loss is at times unbearable, but you can't get stuck there. Reaching out for help and support is a sign of strength. Be open to talking with someone as you go through your grief. Be open to going to counseling so you can obtain the tools to assist you with navigating through these feelings of grief.

Transparency Moment – June 18, 2019
Take Care of You

I must admit the last week and a half have been a bit tough. Whenever you deal with the loss of a loved one or you experience some type of difficulty sometimes you may feel like we are all alone. It feels as if no one around understands, not even the ones closest to you. And in some cases, they don't understand. So, looking at those who don't understand hoping they will understand and comfort you can be frustrating. The best thing to do is talk to God about it. Cast it over to Him. God can comfort through prayer and through His Word. I must add, it is good to talk with someone who has experienced what you're dealing with and has come through and out! And of course, if you need counseling do that too (I'm an advocate for counseling!). Sometimes there are layers of things that must be addressed so you can walk in complete wholeness.

It Taught Me

I realized something else I had not really done through this time of grieving. I haven't pampered or properly taken care of myself. Self-care is sooooooo important. I realize that more and more. You must take care of yourself so you can live in a healthy way, work on your divine assignment and be there for those you love. When you neglect yourself it is symbolic of you saying you don't matter. BUT YOU DO MATTER! Take care of yourself- spiritually, physically, mentally, emotionally, and financially. Take care of you. Enjoy YOU. Pamper yourself, go on vacation, treat yourself special.

So today, I chose to pamper myself. Getting that much needed massage. Thank you, Lord. Next on the list is a getaway! Where are some places that you would like to go? Take some time to think about a mini getaway to help you relax and possibly help to take your mind off things.

Grieving with Grace

During your time of grieving, the last thing you may be thinking about is self-care. But self-care is necessary to maintain your well-being. Initially, all you may want to do is cry. It's okay to cry and let it out. Don't try to be strong for others and show no emotions. Allow yourself to feel what you feel. However, as you grieve, take time to implement self-care. You may need to create a self-care plan. Make sure you eat, rest and do something that you enjoy. Do things that make you smile…again.

What self-care ideas have you done before? Write down some possible self-care options to start your self-care plan.

Transparency Moment – July 2, 2019
Call for Help

I hope to help someone through this. I understand clearly now how some people post about checking on your strong friends. Sometimes the people that hold things together for others can at times become overwhelmed with what they are personally confronted with. I consider myself a strong person. Although, I truly recognize that the strength I possess is truly from God. I draw from His strength and have been doing so for some time. However, the last two weeks in June were a bit tough for me. I felt emotionally drained because not only am I still processing my feelings of grief, but there were also some other things coming at me all at one time and it was draining. It got to the point where I didn't want to go anywhere, talk to anyone, do anything.... just sleep. Yup, I know... the enemy was trying his very best to bring me to a totally depressed state. Some would say that would never happen to them because they are too saved and anointed. I appreciate the strength in you, but sometimes things occur in our lives to bring us places we never thought we would be. Through all of this I have this strong feeling that I had to experience it so I could fully be able to relate to those who I would help. I know that sounds strange, but I do believe God has a plan for me and He is taking me this way for His glory. I must keep telling myself, I will come through this. God allowed me to experience some peace and to do some things that I love to help me through. God knows how to put a smile back on your face to let you know He got you.

It Taught Me

Call for help when you need it. Don't stay there. If you're depressed, discouraged, or overwhelmed, don't stay there. Get the help you need. God never intended for you to remain discouraged. HE WANTS TO GIVE YOU HOPE AND AN EXPECTED END. He has great plans for you.

I remember a scripture that someone shared with me. Proverbs 23:18: For surely there is an end and thine expectation shall not be cut off (paraphrased). Whatever you may be experiencing it will come to an end. Put your expectations in the atmosphere. Be encouraged. Help is on the way!

Grieving with Grace

You can't rush the process of grieving. Everyone moves differently through it. Some would even tell you to get over it. Getting over it is easier said than done. Sometimes outsiders who can't comprehend your pain from your grief belittle your process. Don't let them rush you. Take the time you need to heal.

Don't isolate yourself when you're grieving. Even though you may not necessarily feel like being around people, push yourself to do so. Reach out for help. Go to God in prayer and seek counsel with someone you trust.

Transparency Moment – July 8, 2019
Accept It

On Friday, November 30, 2018, my daughter Crystal was transported from Hospice care to the hospital only because I didn't sign the paperwork that says not to revive her if she's passing (DNR). So, I got the call from Hospice to tell me to report to the hospital. I remember sending a text to my boss to inform her that I had to leave to go to the hospital and that I believed that my daughter was going to pass. She responded by saying stay positive it could be that she is getting better. I responded to her text: "No ma'am. She's going to pass I already know and have accepted it. She has stage 4 cancer, and they aren't going to treat it anymore, but thank you. God got me."

As I think back at this incident and after pondering a few things happening in my life now, these two words jumped in my spirit: ACCEPT IT. I had to accept the fact that I was losing my daughter and there was NOTHING I could do about it. There is no way that I can change the OUTCOME of my daughter's passing. I must ACCEPT IT.

It Taught Me

It also had me thinking about some other things in life. Sometimes no matter how hard we pray about it, cry about it, argue about it, be angry about it, be discouraged about it, or even become depressed about it, there comes a time when we must ACCEPT IT.

When you are in a relationship with someone you love, but they display lack of interest in you and your well-being, and you've tried everything to make that relationship work (as best of your ability and knowledge) and they show you no interest anymore.... ACCEPT IT. You can't make a person love you. That song, "I'm going to make you love me." is crazy. Who wants to spend the rest of their lives MAKING someone love them? When you have a HEAVENLY FATHER that loves you unconditionally and has thoughts of peace and not of evil concerning your life....ACCEPT THAT!!!

Sometimes the connections you've made with others just don't seem to really connect. Let it go.... ACCEPT IT. Sometimes the ideas you had and the plan you had didn't quite work out and you may have become so discouraged about it. Listen, it didn't work out not because you're a failure, but maybe the timing wasn't right, the connections you had at the time wasn't right.

Listen, maybe YOU weren't even right.... ACCEPT IT. ACCEPT IT and move on.

When you can come to grips with things that you have no control over. You can finally ACCEPT IT (surrender to it), then you can pick up the broken pieces, mend, forgive, heal, get delivered, get new direction, and even love again.

Now don't get me wrong, I know there are some things you should not accept, but that's not what this writing is about. It's about accepting some things for what they are and moving on in peace.

Now, I understand the serenity prayer. "God grant me the serenity to ACCEPT the things I cannot change, the COURAGE to change the things I can and the WISDOM to know the difference."

Grieving with Grace

The last stage of the five stages of grief is acceptance. It's when you have finally accepted that your loved one is gone, and you realize it's time to move on with your life. This may take time to get to this stage, but when you get there, you will know because you will allow yourself to accept it and live on. Getting to this stage of acceptance doesn't mean you're happy about your loss or that you have forgotten about your loved one, it simply means that you have come to grips with the loss and are ready to move forward with your life.

Transparency Moment – July 12, 2019
Never Be the Same

About a month or so someone told me after reading one of my posts about the passing of my daughter, Crystal, that I would never be the same. In essence, the old norm is done away with and the new norm is here and now. Those words resonated in my spirit today. "I will never be the same." Did that mean I would always be sad? Did that mean something bad? Did that mean I would never get through this? Would the people around me ever understand my pain? Did that mean I would become better?

Sometimes the greatest struggles, opposition, hardship, disappointment, persecution, pain can present an opportunity for us to be sad, angry, bitter, depressed, stuck, stagnate, lonely and so on. Those feelings and emotions are real, but you can't stay there. You have to come through and you have to come out, you have to decide to be better. You have to boldly say, I will never be the same. This doesn't mean sadness, this means I must rise above what I'm experiencing, tap into God's strength, re-evaluate my life and push forward.... BOLDLY.

It Taught Me

Sometimes going back to the old norm is not the will of God. It's a comfort zone. It's a place of stagnation. Sometimes the push of your pain will propel you to a place that God can ultimately get the glory out of your life.

Yes, some experiences are so painful, discouraging and they look hopeless, but we can't lose hope, and we can't allow those experiences to cause us to give up (Psalm 27:13-14). You must get up from there and tell yourself, I will never be the same, not in a negative way, but from a place of POWER.

When we accept Jesus Christ into our lives and the transformation begins, we can honestly say in some cases that what we used to do, we don't do anymore. In essence, you will never be the same. My life will never be the same.... but I'm okay.

Grieving with Grace

The statement the person told me is true. So, I will share it with you. You will never be the same. When you grieve a loved one, a part of your life will never be the same. Depending on who you lost can impact you in many ways. Some people remain in pain, depression and sadness for the rest of their lives or for many years after the loss. Things will be different, but in time, you will learn to become accustomed to living without them. Breathe. I know that sounds heavy to accept. It may sound like something you wished wasn't true. However, please know that the intensity of your sadness will lessen as the years move forward.

This doesn't mean that you have forgotten about your loved one, it just means the pain of the loss has lessened. You have become accustomed to the new norm. This is usually during the acceptance stage of grief where you can accept the loss and move forward with your life.

Transparency Moment – July 17, 2019
Her Strengths

In the past couple of weeks, I've been exposed to a few things that had me reflecting on some strengths of my daughter. One of her abilities was to be able to hustle. When I mean hustle, I mean she was willing to tap into her talents and find ways to generate income. She had not worked a regular job for years. I know she had been back in SC for over 8 years, and she had not worked a job. She lived on her own and before she died, she was renting a home. She used whatever ability, skill, idea she had within her and then some to earn money to take care of herself and her children. She knew how to make money and to hold onto it. Even after her death, she still had money in her "reserve" account as she called it. I often wondered how she did it. I mean she went on trips, bought stuff for her kids, and made it happen. I often told her that she was blessed and that she had favor. No job, 4 children (and child support wasn't consistent) and she was able to sustain her household financially better than two married people. We often had mini talks (full of laughs) about "two monies" vs. "one money." She often wondered why a married couple couldn't (two monies=income) hold down a home etc. and she was able to with "one money (income)" as a single person. If they got two monies (as she would say), why are they not ahead? Thinking about that conversation makes me laugh now a little, but she was right.

Another strength to describe her is that she had resilience. Merriam-Webster dictionary defines resilience as: the capacity to recover quickly from difficulties and tough times, toughness. Crystal was resilient. She experienced quite a few setbacks, the cancer was the major one, but besides that one she never gave up. She would always bounce back. Even while she was on her first day at Hospice Care, I called her full name and she said, "What is it?" I was like I'm just checking on you and when Poppy and I were getting ready to leave she was trying her best to get out the bed to go home with us (shocked me).

She would find a way to fight through accomplishing what she wanted. She pushed through while trying to overcome obstacles with 4 children (one special needs and the other with a rare/life threatening skin disease). I can remember when her twins were born and Keoni was diagnosed with a rare fatal skin disease (EB). She wasn't giving up on him. They said he wouldn't live to be a year, but the resilience in Crystal and her love for her son literally did everything she could to care for him. I believe she gave him life through her love for him. He has lived beyond a year old and has even lived beyond her. He is still alive and strong today (wow.... the power of love).

I was thinking about her today and her many strengths. I've learned a few things from observing her.

It Taught Me

Hustle - use what talents and gifts you have been given and move with passion towards making them manifest. You have a specific time here on the earth so don't hold back on what you've been given. Crystal didn't hold back. If one thing didn't work, she would quickly seize the opportunity to do something else that would work. You got to know when to seize the moment, seize the opportunity to advance.

I've learned - save your money! Keep a reserve account, don't touch it. Spend wisely and enjoy fun times every now and then with what you've saved.

We must aim to be resilient - giving up is not an option. Tough times come to us all. Some things tougher than most, but it should make you stronger. It's these experiences or opportunities that show us what we are made of and to show us God's power and love.

Grieving with Grace

Maybe there is something significant about the loved one you've lost. Maybe it was something about their character, personality or something they achieved that you could learn something from. Take a moment to think about their good qualities. Think about how they impacted your life. Share and reflect in your journal what you learned from observing them.

Transparency Moment – July 19, 2019
Support of Others

Sometimes when we experience tough times, we need the support of others until we can get through on our own. It's the empathy shown from others that comfort us. It's the love that others show that help us heal. I can remember shortly after my daughter, Crystal's funeral, I was in church, and I was trying so hard to give God praise. I was trying so hard to get into the service, but I just couldn't break free. The pain was too fresh. All I could think about is seeing my daughter in a casket right at the altar at the church I attended. It was hard to shake initially. Sometimes it is still difficult. I even think about her shouting at the altar. For a few weeks after she passed, I would even look back in the congregation looking for her.

Well, it was one Sunday, I was feeling heavy as I said, and it was hard to get into the service. Other people around me were praising God and shouting around. It was that Sunday that a lady in our church must have discerned the heaviness in my spirit. She moved gracefully by me and grabbed my arm and started shouting and I followed along. It was so hard!!! It hurt from my core. All I could do was cry. God this is so hard!!! (My thoughts). The pain was so difficult, but I felt like something broke that day. As I type this now and think about it, the tears are starting to come. I thought about that Sunday, even this morning and I gleaned from it that sometimes we need someone to show the love, empathy, compassion to help us through. She didn't ignore me, but she saw my pain and wanted me out of it. For that I am forever grateful to her for this simple act of love. I'm so appreciative for that lady for being obedient to the leading of God's Spirit.

Another person I know that helped me do something that I just didn't have the courage to do was one of Crystal's best friends from New Jersey (that's not to say others didn't, but these are ones I'm sharing now). I'll share her initials N.P. The very day that Crystal passed (December 2, 2018), I did not have the courage to tell Jasmine that her mother had passed away. Losing your mother is difficult at any age, but when you are young it can be very difficult. I could not tell her. It may have been selfish of me, but at the time I was trying my best to grasp the fact that I just saw my daughter's lifeless body at the hospital just a few hours ago. I couldn't do it. I was able to get to church so I could get some sort of strength to help me through the days, months, and life ahead. I asked her friend if she could please tell Jasmine. I know it was difficult for her too because Crystal was her best friend and her husband, knew Crystal for over 30 years. #68/#64. I am forever grateful for her courage to help share this sad news with Jasmine.

It Taught Me

We have the power to love and when we utilize that power it can heal, mend, deliver, make whole, stabilize, bring peace and so much more to those we release it too.

God may very well lead you to encourage someone. When He does, do it. If He shared it with you, they need it.

There are some people that will be in your corner to help you through until you are able to do so. God sends these people in our path.

Some people are hurting right before us. Sometimes we overlook them, sometimes we talk about them, sometimes we may even joke or discuss their behavior because we don't understand what they are going through. Next time, have empathy. Next time, pray for them. Next time, try to put yourself in their shoes and ask yourself how would you respond? Oftentimes, we are so quick to say we wouldn't act like that or handle it like that. Listen, you don't know what you would do. Next time show God's love.

Grieving with Grace

Sometimes through the grieving process you may feel like you are all alone. You may feel like no one understands your pain. There are some people that are coming in your path to support you through the process. They will provide support, a shoulder to lean on and someone you can talk to. Be open to receive what you need from them. Some have gone through a loss just like you and are ready to share a story, maybe a hug to let you know that you are not alone. You will get through this!!!

Transparency Moment – July 23, 2019
68

I just got back from an amazing time in New Jersey. I was able to go back home! I had not been back home for about 2.5 years. My father had major surgery (2016), which resulted in Crystal and I moving him to South Carolina. The house I knew as home had been up for foreclosure because my dad just couldn't carry the load anymore (it's a long story - he bought it in 1974). We all knew that the days at 68 were over. That was tough for us all to accept, but we had to. Two years after that Crystal I. Garrett was diagnosed with cancer. Her journey to get healed prevented her from visiting NJ like she wanted to. During that time, we heard that 68 was bought and was being remodeled.

This weekend I went to NJ, and I asked one of my friends (GP) to drive me to my old house so I could take pictures of the front of the house to share with my dad. As we were taking pictures, she asked me, "Do you want to go ring the bell?" My eyes lit up and I yelled, "YES!" So, we walked to the pathway leading to the steps to the front door. Before we could get to the top step the owner of the home opened the door. Come to find out, my friend knew the new owner. She introduced me and we asked could he let me in to see what he had done to the home. He opened the door!!! We went in and I began to explain how I grew up there and then I asked if I could please take pictures and record video as long as I didn't post on social media. He allowed me to go all through the house, downstairs, upstairs, backyard and the remodeled attic. My God, it was so beautiful! I cried walking through the house thinking about my childhood, the good memories and I even said I wish Crystal could see this. She loved 68. Even though the home had some major repair issues, it was still home for all of us.

I am so thankful today to be able to walk in that home again and see how it was remodeled. I am thankful that God strategically ordered my steps that day, had me call the right friend to pick me up so that the connection could be made. I am forever grateful. I know that was God!

It Taught Me

God is amazing. He will strategically set things up for you that are a part of your heart's desire. God knew I wanted to get in that house. He knew exactly who should take me to get in. All I had to do was follow and once the opportunity appeared…go in BOLDLY and with HUMILITY.

I also glean from this situation that the doors are open. The doors will open for you. Put your request before the

Lord, leave it alone and trust that He will do it for you. Before we knocked, the owner opened the door. That's exactly how God wants to do it for you, before you even realize it.... THE DOOR WILL OPEN.

Grieving with Grace

During the grieving process there may be places that remind you of your loved one. Sometimes it's places that you've travelled to, places you used to go to or places where you used to live. If you have access to those places, it's good to take time to visit those places on behalf of your loved ones.

Reminisce on the good times together and every so often go to those places and/or do those things in their honor.

Transparency Moment – July 27, 2019
Advocate

While in New Jersey, I had dinner with a friend of mine while I was there. We had a good time together talking and catching up. It had been well over ten years since I'd seen her last. We got into a discussion about her experience with cancer and the difficulty of obtaining disability to assist during her treatment. I then began to share with her that my daughter had applied for disability a couple of months prior to her passing. When she applied, she was in desperate need of funds to sustain her household obligations and to provide for her children. I remember that she told me while she was in the hospital that the disability department told her that she was denied her request. I said to her, "How can they deny you when you are truly in need of the help?" She went on to say that they denied her because she shared that someone helped her financially one time and they couldn't give her money because of that. I was like, but other people are not going to always give you money - you legitimately need the help. I'm still trying to process how they denied an individual that had a terminally ill disease with four children. WOW. How could this be? Then she shared that they not only denied her, but they took away the disability that her son was receiving as well. All while she was in the hospital trying to fight to LIVE.

As I heard my friend's story and remembering Crystal's situation being similar with applying for disability, I thought to myself there has got to be some form of advocacy. Because if they went through it, there are probably a whole lot of other people experiencing it too. I know there are some who abuse the system, but my daughter needed that help, and it hurts to know that she was denied simply because someone gave her some money for her rent.

It Taught Me

I looked up the word in the Merriam-Webster's dictionary, ADVOCATE: A person who publicly supports or recommends a particular cause or policy. Everyone has been put on the earth for a divine purpose. We all have an assignment. We are all here to advocate for something. It could be Christianity, Women's Rights, Domestic Violence, Cancer Awareness, the Power of Fatherhood, Teen mothers, preventing gun violence, mentoring youth and the list goes on. We must stand and support something. It is part of the reason for our existence. It's beyond us, it's for a greater good. What will you stand for? What will you support? What impact will you make in the lives of others? Who or what are you advocating for? It's truly something to think about. It truly has been on my mind stronger since my daughter's death. Ask God to guide you as to where and in what capacity that you can make a greater impact for the glory of God. Blessings!

Grieving with Grace

Sometimes people have lost loved ones because of something tragic, and it moves them so much not only because of the death, but also the way the death occurred. Some people have lost loved ones from cancer, gang violence, gun violence, domestic violence, drunk drivers, swimming accidents and the list goes on and those kinds of deaths sometimes have a specific movement or organization that advocates for those kinds of losses.

During this process, you may want to become a part of a support group or organization that advocates and supports the kind of loss your loved one experienced. There may be some kind of advocacy, foundation, scholarship fund or non-profit organization that you may want to start on their behalf. Doing something in their honor and to advocate for others just like them will provide support for you and also some kind of fulfillment to mend the pain of your loss during the grieving process. Who will you advocate for?

Transparency Moment – August 1, 2019
The Cell Phone

The other day my father wanted to purchase a new phone and go with another phone carrier because he thought he was going to get an upgrade on his phone. I kept saying why don't you just stay with the same company, and you can get a phone through them. All he really wanted was to make sure that when he called from his phone that it said his name. The way it was set up, it had my daughter's name on the caller id. I kept saying stay with the same company and he asked me why? I simply said, "I still have Crystal's phone." He said, "Why do you still need her phone? Let's just shut it off so I could pay less." I froze. Couldn't answer him. He asked again, "Why do you need her phone?" I answered quickly, "There's stuff on it I need to get...." My sentenced trailed off. I froze because I knew I was not ready to release her phone. I know that sounds strange. It's not like I'm using it, or people are really calling on it (except bill collectors). There is a bit of information on it that I probably will need, but I don't really need the phone. I froze because a part of me doesn't want to let go, and her phone is a form of connection to her. After my father asked me about the phone, I didn't realize that is what I felt deep inside, I DON'T WANT TO LET GO. I'm asking God to help me. I'm not out of touch with reality. I know Crystal is with

God and I know I won't see her again on this side of Heaven, but some of her items I just can't part with just yet.

It Taught Me

There may be some experiences, some toxic people (connections) that you don't want to let go of, but by holding onto them you stagnate your growth, you block yourself from healthy relationships. Sometimes when we don't want to let go it's because the wound still needs to heal. Not letting go and releasing it to God slows down that healing process. Some connections need to be severed for the sake of your wholeness, peace, and your overall wellbeing.

Now don't get me wrong, there are some things we should hold onto as a keepsake from family members to share the history, but in my case it's not the phone.

What are some of things or people that you are holding onto that God has told you to release? God asked Samuel, how long will you mourn after Saul...." - I'm convinced that there is a time to let go and to release it over to the Lord.

Grieving with Grace

During this grieving process, you may not want to part with some of the belongings of your loved ones. I've even heard about how some people leave the rooms of their loved ones the same. Maybe that's you. Some people shift things to the garage, attic, or basement. Some of my daughter's things are still in my garage today. So, I get it. However, it's important to let some things go. Take the time to release some items that are not necessary to keep. Some things you will need to let go of. Set a time to do so. This may not happen right away but set time to let those things go little by little.

Transparency Moment – August 5, 2019
Acts of Faith Tour

I had the privilege of going to see Iyanla Vanzant for her Acts of Faith tour in Columbia, SC. I purchased a copy of her original purple book, Acts of Faith back in the 80s. It was such a source of encouragement and motivation. I was thrilled to hear that she would be in town and that the tour would be based on the book. I purchased the new copy because I like to support other authors because I want to be supported as well.

There were so many powerful nuggets shared that night. She shared about the caterpillar and its transformation into a butterfly. The caterpillar doesn't exactly know what's going on, but something on the inside tells it it's time to change. It's time to shift into something different.

One of the statements that Ms. Vanzant shared that night was that her daughter died at age 31. I thought, wow. She can identify with the pain I'm feeling. I later read that her daughter died on Christmas Day to cancer. That night Ms. Vanzant shared that when she lost her daughter, she went INSANE for 3 YEARS! When the words rolled off her tongue into the atmosphere, I froze. She shared that it was tough for her. I thought 3 YEARS!!! Wow....then I read that she went into a depression. She wanted to even commit suicide. My God! But then I noticed something else......she came through it and now she's in a position and platform that is aimed to empower people.

It Taught Me

There are certain rooms, atmospheres, environments, certain people you need to connect to for you to grow. Sometimes you really have to step out of your comfort zone. In doing so it will help you to get what you really need to push you to find the missing piece of your purpose. Sometimes in those rooms, at those conferences, in those atmospheres and around those people are really where you can grow.

The caterpillar knows there is a need for change. Sometimes you can recognize the need for change when you become restless, frustrated with how things are, feelings of unfulfillment and inwardly yearning for something different. Your spirit recognizes there is a need for change. A need to shift, a need to move forward. Recognize it. Embrace it and walk in that change. The outcome of your obedience is going to be phenomenal #AwakenHER

When I heard that Iyanla Vanzant lost her daughter to cancer, my immediate thoughts went to me losing my daughter who was only 36. When she said she went INSANE for 3 years, I thought WOW! I realized then that it is a process to heal from grieving. I also realized that her story would NOT be my story. As I sat in my seat that night, I decided that my daughter's death would not take me off course. I would not go INSANE. I would not allow it to stop me from doing and fulfilling the assignment that God has for my life. I'M ALIVE!!! Yes, I will miss her and will process this through with the help of God, but I will not go insane, nor will I even think about suicide. I will use what has happened to bring glory to God. I will use what happen to her to be an advocate for people like her. (Connections Impacted by Grace Community Development Corp – CIGCDC).

Even though Iyanla experienced setbacks, she pushed through, and God opened a platform for her to empower others. I will push through. YOU will push through. Whatever situations you may have encountered, allow what happened to propel you right into your divine assignment. God has a plan, and it will amaze you if you allow Him to reveal it to you.

Grieving with Grace

You may feel so empty on this journey of grief. Possibly having feelings of depression and sadness, but don't allow those emotions to overtake you. If you feel like your emotions are overtaking you, seek out the help you need. Talk with someone, seek counsel, pray. Don't consider taking your own life, you have so much more to fulfill. Even though the pain feels unbearable at times, you will come through this. Seek help, seek support from others you love if you are truly feeling overwhelmed. Do what you need to do to bring balance to yourself so you can gain the strength you need to move forward.

Transparency Moment – August 9, 2019
I was Angry

I knew I initially had those feelings, but I had never said it out of my mouth until last night. Now, I know some may take this the wrong way, but I felt it. I didn't stay there, but I initially was angry with God, more so disappointed/hurt about my daughter passing away. It happened so fast. Before I could get a grip as to what was happening to her....it was happening, and it happened fast. She was dying. I held those feelings inside for a few months (February 2019). I could remember hearing other people share about their miracles and how God turned the situation around for them. I can remember one woman of God sharing how her son was near death and she prayed and believed God and God raised him up. As I listened, I was happy to hear the testimonies, but inwardly I was struggling because I had hoped that God would have done that for Crystal. Now, I understand the attacks of the enemy and how spiritual warfare worked as well as knowing that God doesn't put sickness on us, but I was also fully aware that God had the power and ability to work a miracle. And I was trying to figure out why God didn't do it for Crystal in that manner.

I can remember sitting in church during Sunday school and the thoughts of being disappointed about Crystal's outcome got heavy on me. So heavy, that I sent a text to a preacher friend of mine to release what I felt. "Why did she have to die? Couldn't God just turn it around? Why?" These were the questions that I sent that morning. The person quickly reminded me not to put the blame on God. I had to keep the right posture and the right attitude. I had to give God praise that my daughter was out of pain, and she made it into Heaven. That was my prayer, God don't let Crystal go to Hell. And even in her death there was several people that surrendered their life to God during her Homegoing service (funeral). She really touched so many lives. After reading the words from the text, I had to shift my thoughts and not be angry with God about anything.

It Taught Me

My anger, my disappointment had to turn quickly because I knew I needed the power of God to get me through my process. How can I be angry with the one that would see me through? I had to shift. The Bible says we can be angry (Ephesians 4:26) if we don't allow it to turn to sin. I was glad that my preacher friend quickly reminded me to change my attitude.

Sometimes we can put the best face forward. We can act like everything is great, but inwardly there are some struggles that fight us. Let me help you, it's best to address, confront and release those inward struggles so that God can begin the healing process. When we hold it in, it comes out in other ways that may not be as positive. Be honest with God about how you feel about things. He knows already, He just wants to hear from you. When we're honest about it, then God can heal us from it. He is so AMAZING!

Sometimes we are not going to understand why things happen the way they do. Sometimes we're not going to understand why we had to lose a loved one, but we must realize that we can't stay here (physically). We all must walk the journey from life to death. The key to it all is to make sure that you are connected to God throughout your life. The key is to make sure that you are saved and have accepted Jesus Christ as Lord. The key is to live your life to the fullest for God's glory. Crystal knew God, ran from God, rebelled, and returned back to God just in time for her to make it in. I will say this, every case is different. If I were you, I wouldn't play with your walk with God or act like you don't need God, you need Him! Don't risk not having Him in hopes that you can later run to Him when you are at your dying bed. Crystal knew she needed God. She also knew (as she testified in church) that she was out there and was far from God - she realized she opened the door for the enemy. Don't let that be your story.... turn to God NOW. If she were here, I'm sure she would say the same.

Grieving with Grace

There may be times when you may feel angry that your loved one is no longer here. If anger is the feeling you have, feel it. However, don't allow yourself to remain there. It will only hinder your grieving process towards healing from it all. Being angry is not going to bring them back. Your loved one would want you to live a life of peace and to fulfill your purpose in life. Don't waste days being filled with anger. Cherish the good memories they left you with and allow that to bring a calm to you.

Transparency Moment – August 19, 2019
Stabilize Yourself First

Well, the summer break is over for me, and everyone is getting prepared for this new school year. Both my boys are in college and Jasmine (my granddaughter) will be a junior in high school and the twins will be going to the 1st grade and Nicole is living with her dad and paternal grandmother. Today I reflect on June 2019 when my granddaughter, Jasmine, went to be with her dad for the summer. I was glad she did so that she could possibly bond with her dad to help her process her mother's death. Not only that, I needed time to process my daughter's passing as well. I know that Jasmine wanted to come back home to my house (the new norm for her), but each time she mentioned it I kept saying let's wait. Didn't know it was going to be the week leading up to school, but I'm glad it was. I needed that time. I honestly was not emotionally prepared to help her through her process as I was trying so hard to get through myself. I needed time to regroup. My boys also needed that space as they prepared for college.

Yesterday she returned and I was excited to see her. As I hugged her in church, I felt like I was ready. I'm ready to guide her through this next phase in her life.

Some may consider me selfish for not letting her come back in the summer, but I experienced so many different feelings throughout that timeframe that I look back now, and I believe I made the right choice. I had to process things myself. It reminds me of something they tell you while on the airplane to prepare you in the event of a crash. They tell you to first put on your oxygen mask and then assist your children. They tell you this so that you can stabilize yourself so that you will be able to help your children/family that are with you. So, I needed that time to help stabilize me. In Luke 22, Jesus tells Peter that when he is converted, then go back and strengthen your brother.

It Taught Me

You know, we must be honest enough to say, I'm not strong enough for that right now. Or I'm not ready/prepared for that right now. It's not to say you won't ever be because if you lean on God and follow His direction you're bound to be strong enough, prepared enough and ready enough to do whatever He is assigning for your life.

Backing up and taking this time to regroup has helped me tremendously. I feel stronger and for that I am so grateful. It's okay to take time for yourself; actually, it's necessary.

Put your mask on first. Get you right first. Stabilize you first. Get your business straight first. Get your prayer life straight first. You must do it because there are so many lives connected to you that will need you at your best. You need to be at your best for YOU and for those you will impact.

Grieving with Grace

At some point you will need to take time for yourself. This may mean you might have to separate yourself for a moment to help stabilize your feelings and emotions. Pull away to regain your strength again. Communicate your needs to others you care about, so they won't be concerned about you going into depression. Communicate with your family what you are feeling and help them to understand to allow you time to get yourself together. Stabilize yourself first. How will you begin the process of stabilizing yourself first? Share your thoughts with someone or write them out in a journal.

Transparency Moment – August 22, 2019
Connected

Yesterday was the twins' birthday and I had picked up Jasmine from where she was and took her to stop by to visit with them. They were excited to see her. They hadn't really seen her all summer because she was away with her dad. As she and I talked with them in their room, I noticed pictures of my daughter, **Crystal**. The first one I noticed was on a blanket that their father made with all her pictures so the twins could always remember their mother. I saw her face on that blanket and I froze. It was like she was looking directly at me. Then I looked up on their wall and there were more pictures of her. The children kept talking about their toys and they seemed fine, but I got stuck a little. I then told Jasmine to look. She did and then she froze a little. She quickly tried to get me to change the subject. I did, but inwardly I was struggling. I know the children are fine, but I just know Crystal would have loved to enjoy their birthday with them. Crystal used to go all out for birthday parties for her children.

I noticed that Kymani didn't want Jasmine to leave her at all. I believe that Jasmine is her closest connection to her mom. Keoni gave me a long hug. He held me tight and hugged me for a long time. I felt his love. I can remember Crystal telling me while she was sick in the hospital to make sure I got close and stayed close to Jasmine. She said, not because I'm sick, but she needs that connection. Little did we know there was a real reason why she said that because after her death, Jasmine would be living with me. We're probably helping each other more than we know. She needs me and I need her.

It Taught Me

I realize all of this is a process and it just doesn't go away when you get up the next day. People we love and who we've been connected to are with us for a lifetime. In some way they have impacted us. In some way we have impacted them. What we've learned from them will be with us forever. Sometimes the connection is needed to get someone through certain seasons in their lives. Sometimes your connection brings joy, peace, and comfort to another. Sometimes a connection from someone else brings comfort to you. Keoni's hug brought comfort to me.

Think about some of the connections you made through your life. What connections have been good for you? Who are you connected with that you bring comfort to?

Grieving with Grace

If the pain of your loss makes you feel hopeless, don't allow yourself to remain in that state of mind. Allow yourself to experience the emotion so you can heal, but don't stay there long. Believe it or not, life and people are continuing to move around you. Sometimes you may have to connect with others that will help you get through and cope through your grief. This may mean that you will have to talk with someone you trust. You may also need to visit a therapist to help you process the pain. I mention this quite a few times so as to prepare you for it. Sometimes connecting to a counselor to help you process the pain is necessary. It's okay to do that. Doing so will help mend your heart. This will help you later when you begin to connect with others you will impact. Let me inform you that during your grief, you are here for a reason and a purpose and there is something for you to accomplish. God will connect you with your purpose as you all Him to guide you through your new norm. There is a story for you to tell so you can't get stuck in the pain of your loss.

Transparency Moment – August 28, 2019
Fifteen

As I looked through my wallet and noticed I had my daughter, Crystal's graduation picture, it brought back some memories. She looked so pretty. Then I looked at the most recent picture of me and Jasmine and it brought back some memories as well. Memories of how this all started. I can remember being 15 years old and having a child. I had no clue about how to handle being pregnant at 15, having a baby or even about sex for that matter. Wow....as I think about it, I was so young, naive, and immature. Yet, I was pregnant with a child that I really didn't want. That may sound harsh, but at 15, no one wants to have a baby. You got dreams of your own, or at least at that age your parents have dreams for you. Prior to me having Crystal, my parents discussed with me the possibility of adoption. They felt it would be best because I was so young, and they wanted me to continue my teenage years free from the major responsibility of being a mother (I knew nothing!). So, we told the doctor I would be giving this child up for adoption.

However, as soon as I gave birth to Crystal, the doctor laid her right on my chest. Now, you know it's hard for a mother (no matter what age) to hold their baby and let it go...a connection was established. So, when it came time for me to leave the hospital, my parents came in the room and asked about the adoption. I began to cry and said, "I can't do it." The love connection between Crystal and I had begun. So, my parents said they would help and that there was no way they would separate a mother from her child. Hmmmmm....as I think about this there is so much to tell between what happened that day and what happened the day we had to separate.

I look back at that time I can remember how embarrassing and shameful it was to be pregnant and to have a child at such a young age. I felt ashamed for me and for my family. At that time there were only 2 girls pregnant at our high school. I was one of them. Times have changed because we see this happening way too many times. As I began to search my heart, I later realized that the spirit of shame has followed me into my adulthood. That spirit is deep.... I did a whole talk about it in my book, Loving Who I Am ~ Inside and Out (GET A COPY!)

As I looked at her picture and the picture of me and Jasmine, I thought about what happened when Crystal was pregnant with Jasmine. Crystal already had Nicole so she didn't think she could raise Jasmine too so she and I talked about adoption (wow....look at how history repeats itself - cycles). So, I found a Christian couple through a Pastor's wife that I knew (I won't name her or them) and we talked about the couple adopting Jasmine (they had another name for her), but something happened. Like I said, history at times repeats itself. I knew Crystal was going to go through adoption, so she didn't see or hold her baby. However, I think I had the same feelings when I had Crystal. I went to the hospital and I said, "Don't do it. We will figure it out." Then I asked the nurse to bring Jasmine in....and that was all it took. Crystal and Jasmine's love connection began. They were close just like Crystal and I were. Little did we know, that Jasmine would be the one that would help take care of her mother. And little did I know, that when Jasmine turned 15 (history again) that I would be taking care of her. (Wow). During the time of Crystal's illness, she told me, "Ma, you need to get closer to Jasmine." Now I understand that statement a whole lot more.

It Taught Me

We all have a story to tell. There are some things you've experienced that may be shameful to you but need to be told to help another. You didn't go through it just for you. Yes, your stories (experiences) have taught you many things, but they will also help others too, if you tell it. You can't change the past, but you can change your future so hold your head up.

Make a connection with your children. Don't let anything or anyone sever that connection. Love and forgive. Let old stuff go and love them and teach them how to love and respect you.

There is a girl, a boy, a cousin, a grandson/daughter that needs you. They need your wisdom, your listening ear, your laughter, your discipline, they need you. Do your best to be there for someone that needs you the most. Possibly consider mentoring.

Grieving with Grace

During this time, you may reflect on the connection you have with your loved one. There is something about them that you will never forget. Share those moments with those that remain with you. What you are feeling now is hard, but with time, you will be able to share with another how you pushed through. As time moves forward, you will find yourself being a source of strength for another.

Transparency Moment – September 9, 2019
Her Body is Tired

"She tried her best to fight this thing as long as she could, but her body is tired." These were the words that I shared with Jasmine as she looked at her mother's frail body lying on the hospital bed. We had visited with her mother about 2 weeks prior to that, but Crystal was not responsive. At that time, Jasmine spoke to her mom and Crystal looked at her as if she didn't know who she was and then she slightly smiled and said, "How are you doing?" At this point Crystal's memory was failing her due to the cancer that had spread to her brain. My God. So, when I shared these words with Jasmine at this visit, she was looking at her mother's body almost lifeless.

I remember not really wanting to tell Jasmine that her mother was indeed dying. I went to pick her up from school during her ROTC practice and I said we must go see your mother now. She looked at me and got in the car and said, "What's wrong?" I said, "You need to see your mother." She immediately began to cry and said, "DON'T TELL ME THAT!!!" I didn't have it in me to tell her anything, much less to tell her that it might be the last time she sees her mother alive. I responded, "I'M NOT GOING TO TELL YOU ANYTHING! I need you to just see your mother." I knew once she saw her, she would know. So, when we got in that hospital room, she knew....

It was a shock to her because Crystal's body had changed so much, so quickly. So, as she and I and a few others in the room leaned over Crystal's bed, I said, "She tried her best to fight this thing as long as she could, but her body is tired." That was a hard day also.

It Taught Me

I glean from this incident: Sometimes we fight so hard to MAKE things work. We put in all our energy and efforts to do all we know to do to make something work out the way we think it should. There is nothing wrong with working towards something you believe in or want, but sometimes what we want and what God wants is two different things. After we've done all, we could do, we just need to yield to God. We need to just surrender to His plan and purpose for our lives. The more we try to have a tug-a-war with God, the more we will waste time.

Initially, surrendering is not easy because it involves you taking somewhat of a back seat. It requires the old cliche, "Let Go and Let God." It requires trust. Surrendering brings peace. What have you not surrendered to God yet? I'm in the process of working through this myself. So, I get it if you are uncertain of what will happen if you really, I mean really, give it over to God. Just know that He has your best interest at heart. Allow God to work in your life.

Grieving with Grace

Sometimes we must accept the result. Even though there are times that an outcome is not what we hoped for. You may have hoped and prayed for your loved one to live, but unfortunately, they didn't. I want to say, I'm so sorry. I'm not sure of the cause of death, but possibly it could have been that their body could not undergo anymore pain or the trauma it went through any longer.

Sometimes it has nothing to do with a prolonged sickness, but a sudden, untimely occurrence that took your loved one's life. This can be hard to process because you didn't get to share final words. Allow yourself time to heal from this because it may have been very traumatic for you. My prayer is that God will comfort you during this time. *Matthew 5:4* "Blessed are those who mourn for they shall be comforted."

Transparency Moment – September 17, 2019
God Showed Me

God showed it to me. You know sometimes when God shows you some things, they are not always as pleasant as we would like them to be. However, I believe that He does this at times to help prepare us, to work out some things and to stand in faith - covering the situation in prayer, in hopes that things would change. God is amazing in that He will make you aware of what you need to know. I can remember some time before my daughter, Crystal shared with me about her first diagnosis with cancer that I had a dream that she had died. Now, of course when I had the dream it was indeed scary to me because it seemed so real. I immediately began to bind it up, yet as she went through her process, the dream would play back in my mind. I can distinctly remember Crystal asking me while she was going through chemo and her treatments, "Ma, God didn't show you anything about me? You hear from God. What's He saying?" As she asked that, I knew what God showed me, but I DID NOT want to say what God showed me. I didn't want to put it in the atmosphere. I was remaining positive in hopes that it would not be the case. As time progressed, I knew it was going to happen just as God showed me.

As Crystal went through her process of trying to fight this vicious cancer disease, her body began to decline. Her first surgery, I considered a success because she came through it. It was indeed a struggle for her, and she was in so much pain as she underwent radiation. We were so excited when she finally rang the bell. Then a week later after doing so, the results came back about the cancer spreading. I remember so vividly that on September 6, 2018 - she did her first round of chemo and let me tell you, shortly after that it was downhill from there. Her body rejected the chemo so badly. The dream played back in my head, but I kept praying and then asking God, please don't let Crystal die and go to hell. She had made her peace with God and she and I were able to make peace too. I will never forget her. I know never is a strong word, but I can say, I will NEVER forget her because it's very difficult to forget someone that you gave birth to.

It Taught Me

I share this because sometimes God will show you things ahead of time to prepare you for what is to come. This doesn't always have to be bad stuff (or things that may disturb you naturally) because God shows some good stuff too. But in this instance, He was making me aware so I wouldn't be in complete shock when it finally occurred. I still at times can't believe that she is gone. She was so lively, full of energy, had many gifts and talents.

Although, I may never understand why all this happened, I am grateful that God showed me, and that God has Crystal in glory with Him. God gave her enough time to get her life in order with Him.

Have a listening ear and keep your eyes open because God will reveal exactly what He wants you to know. He doesn't want you to be confused about anything. Nor does He want you to be caught off guard. Acknowledge Him and He will direct you (Proverbs 3:5-6). Disclaimer: every dream about someone dying is not necessarily what's going to happen so be calm. Ask God to make things clear to you. Keep praying - never stop doing that no matter what you've been shown. God thinks highly of you to reveal what He shows you and that is indeed a blessing.

Grieving with Grace

As I shared that God showed me ahead of time that my daughter would pass away. I'm not sure if this happened to you or not. Sometimes knowing ahead of time doesn't necessarily make the grieving process easier. It may help to prepare you, but you will still find yourself going through the grieving process, possibly the same as if you didn't know. It doesn't take away the sadness you may feel. Were you aware of what was going to happen with your loved one or were you completely shocked? Reflect about this and journal your experience and how you feel about it.

Transparency Moment – September 19, 2019
Be the Bridge

I knew something didn't seem right. When I talked with Jasmine last night, she was sharing about a school ring that she wanted to purchase. The juniors were having a meeting today and she wanted me to be aware of it. She was excited, but when I glanced at her I noticed she had this small ring on her finger. My mind immediately went to Crystal. I believe this was a ring that Crystal used to wear. Later that evening I was doing some work on the computer with my husband and Jasmine was upstairs in her room, but for some reason I felt her (my spirit man felt her). I didn't know what she was doing at the time because I was downstairs, but I felt her. So, I sent her a text, "Are you alright." She responded, "Yea." Right after I finished on the computer, I called Jasmine on the phone and said come downstairs. She brought down her information about her school ring. She mentioned that she wanted to put her mother's birthstone on it and then she wanted to put a cancer ribbon on it. I froze for a moment. I knew where we were going with this, and I was wondering whether she was going to be able to handle it and I wondered if I would either. So, I said, "Jasmine, I got to ask you something, but I don't want to make you cry. Are you okay?" So, then it all spilled out...."I was crying upstairs because I really wanted to get a ring, but I wanted to remember my mommy...." and more tears came. All I could do is hug her and say, "I'm so sorry you have to go through this. But you are doing really good, Jasmine and your mother would be very proud of you." The tears stopped, she calmed down, we chatted a little more and then she told me she loved me, and I told her the same.

You must be sensitive to the spirit of God. God will place someone on your heart. He will give you an unction when someone is in need. We must be sensitive to His promptings. Sometimes all you can do for someone is listen. Sometimes just a hug and a few kind words will soothe someone else's pain.

We will never forget Crystal...never. However, during what we may be experiencing to cope - we will grow, we will become stronger, we will advocate for others who have suffered like she suffered. My love for my daughter runs deeper and goes beyond death.

It Taught Me

Be open to be helpful to someone who needs a bridge to cross over. They can walk, but they just need a bridge to get them across to what God has for their lives. A bridge to help them receive the inner healing that God has to offer them. Be a bridge. I know bridges (naturally) are walked on, trampled on, driven on, but it doesn't take away their significance. The bridge is significant in aiding you to get to the destination you are anticipating. Be the bridge.

Grieving with Grace

Amid your grieving process, you will need support to help you through this journey. You can't walk this one alone and please don't try. Reach out to your support systems. The symbolism of the bridge could very well be the time you spend in therapy, talking with a loved one, or obtaining spiritual guidance through a Pastor. Whatever your bridge looks like, get on it, tap into it and walk gracefully to your destination of acceptance and comfort.

Transparency Moment – September 26, 2019
Time is a Treasure

Time is a treasure. Truly a blessing from God. Growing up you think you have plenty of it and as you get older you realize that time is valuable and must be used wisely. Some of us waste so much time on things that really aren't as important as we think. I am thinking of my daughter, Crystal, today because I realize that she and I had wasted a lot of time not doing what mothers and daughters do. Moving to South Carolina was an adjustment for both of us. While navigating through a new living environment, a new set of rules and adapting to me being married, at times it formulated some division between my daughter and me. Listen, sometimes blended families can be difficult to blend, but not impossible if all parties involved have a plan to do so. So, if you are a blended family or considering marrying someone with children, talk things through and determine what things will look like for your relationship and the children you bring to the table. Despite all of that, my daughter and I both loved each other so much. Prior to her older teenage years, we were inseparable. When you saw me, you saw her, but somehow through the course of time things changed. I changed. She changed, but inwardly the love never changed. Even though circumstances might have occasionally fractured our love, it was still there.

This is something that I truly regret (but I have forgiven myself). We allowed the pain of the past to steal precious time together. I recall prior to her preparing for chemo that she wanted to go on this trip together. We were planning a trip and Jasmine was going to go along with us. We had never really taken a trip alone together; it was always with other family members. This time it would be us. However, when it came time for us to go, I was not able to go. I knew she was ill, but I just thought we would have TIME to do that again. However, I was so wrong. Aww, Crystal I am so sorry (ugh, the tears). At the last minute, I said I'll go, but when I reached out, she had already left and was not willing to turn around. I can remember Jasmine trying to convince her to turn around, but she didn't. She was too upset about it, but she forgave me, and we moved on to making sure she was getting the care she needed to fight this disease. However, I am glad that she and Jasmine were able to take that trip together.

As time progressed, we got a chance to work some things out. We made our peace, but I realized that we wasted so many years of focusing on what wasn't right that we failed to work on making things right.

It Taught Me

Value the time you are given because it is a treasure. God has given you a specific time here on earth to fulfill His purpose. Yes, you can enjoy our time here and engage in great relationships, but ultimately, you have something to do for HIM. Don't take it lightly but get connected with the Father and get the understanding of what HIS will is for your life.

Take, make, arrange, set up TIME with those that you love. Don't put off and say we'll do it later or we'll do it when we have more money, or we'll do it when this happens or that happens or when we finish this or when they get through that.... NOPE....DO IT NOW! We are involved in relationships with people that we love and who love us, and we show that expression of love when we spend time with each other. When you spend time with those you love, you show them that you value who they are. If someone really loves you and values the relationship, you're both in, they will spend time with you. Sometimes our focus and priorities are on the wrong things, the wrong people. Check your circle. Love your family, your children, your spouse, your in-laws, your friends. Don't let anything block you from staying connected to those healthy, loving relationships.

What I'm about to share with you right now is very important. Take time for YOURSELF! You are a priority. You matter. You can't neglect yourself and expect to win in any area of your life. If you are a person that everyone relies on, YOU BETTER TAKE CARE OF YOU. The "Me TIME" we hear others say is so important. I see this in my life more so now than ever before. I recognize that I have neglected me and when I look back, I must ask myself, "For what? For whom? For...why?" And when I take self-inventory, I realize that I have wasted so much time being concerned about others that I have overlooked myself. You need TIME to reflect, TIME to heal, TIME to restore yourself back to where God sees you, TIME to spend with God in prayer, TIME to grow and develop. Value your time...it's a treasure.

<u>Grieving with Grace</u>

I'm sure that time with your loved one has been memorable. Reflect on the good times that you all shared. Treasure those moments. Those memories will always be with you. Be sure to take time for those family and friends that remain. Maybe there are some traditions that you kept with your loved one. How can you continue with those family traditions? Make sure you take time for yourself. Implement self-care as often as you can. Be sure to take time for those family and friends that remain.

Transparency Moment – October 9, 2019
I Don't Like It

I don't like it. No matter what way I look at it, I don't like it. However, through the months I've come to accept the fact that Crystal is gone, and she is well. I know that may sound strange because to the natural eyes it's obvious that she's gone, but to really accept it and be at peace with it is two different things. I think I've been up and down with the 5 stages of grief. I've been angry, depressed, bargained, been in denial and I'm moving into acceptance, but that doesn't mean that I like it. Sometimes when I'm in the house and I think about her the tears want to come and sometimes they do, but other times I stomp my feet and say, "God, I don't like this." And then after I've had my moment, I realize that I must accept what has taken place and come to grips that it's not my fault. I know that may sound strange, but at one point I thought I was at fault for her sickness and death. Did I do all that I was supposed to do? Should I have prayed more? There were a lot of different emotions racing through my mind. Someone recently had to reassure me that it wasn't my fault at all. Sometimes so many emotions come to surface when you are experiencing tough times. It's important to lean on God for balance and peace. Some things we just cannot change. It's final. There's no turning back.

It Taught Me

There are some things in life that we are not going to like. No matter how we look at it, we don't like it. We might have felt it was unfair, we weren't treated properly, we felt others didn't value who we were, and the list goes on. However, no matter what happens we can't stay in the negative emotion of what we don't like. Some things we just cannot change, but we can change/adjust our reaction and response to what has happened.

Be honest with God on how you feel. I found this to be so liberating for me. When I'm honest with God about what is happening and how I feel about it (He already knows anyway), then God can heal me at that point and begin the new work in me.

Stop blaming yourself for things you have no control over. For years I blamed myself for why the relationship with my daughter turned sour. And she at times would blame me too, but I realized that there was nothing I could do to change our past, but I wanted so much to create new memories that were positive. Sometimes we were able to do that and then some days the old hurt would surface up again within her and we would be divided again. I'm glad we were able to resolve some of it before her passing. As I look back now and realize that we wasted so much time. Please forgive the ones you say you love. It's not worth forfeiting the time to create new memories. I know I've said this many times, but I can't emphasize that enough. Please forgive them and let it go. When those that hurt you come to apologize, accept their apology, and forgive. If it still hurts, ask God to heal you from that pain. You can't stay in that pain (unforgiveness). You'll wonder why things are not progressing in your life and it could very well be what you are holding against someone that hurt you. Let it go.... please.

Don't let your emotions take control. Don't. Your emotions will change a lot, but you can't be led by them. Ask God for balance so you can be led by His spirit and not a bucket of emotions.

Grieving with Grace

Through your grieving process, there are going to be times when you won't like the fact that your loved one is gone. It's normal to feel that way because you miss them not being in your life. Give yourself time to process everything. If you need to cry, stomp your foot or scream to the top of your lungs, do so. Allow yourself to feel your feelings but do what's necessary to push yourself through them. Feel free to seek help from friends and family for comfort as well.

Transparency Moment – October 17, 2019
The Hospice Experience

Sometimes people don't understand why you feel what you feel when you feel it (I know that's a lot). Things may happen, someone may say something, you may see something that causes a feeling to appear. And even though you try your best to push it back, pack it down and wear a smile on your face...the feeling is still there. Some days are simply AMAZING and then there are days that certain things are said, certain things happen, or I see something that reminds me of my daughter, Crystal and certain feelings/emotions come to surface. (Ugh....it still hurts at times). The other day, I found myself driving by her old residence, parking my car and just sitting there looking at the house. A part of me was wishing she would come out of the house like she used to (LORD HELP). Sometimes it's heavy y'all, but I know God got me.... I'm going to be just fine.

I got a call today from the Hospice company that serviced Crystal prior to her death. They have been trying to reach out to me since her death for a means of support, but I have resisted every time. Today, hearing the voicemail caused some feelings and emotions to emerge. There is a part of me that hates the outcome. There is a part of me that still hurts (tears) and I try my best to be strong (by the grace of God), but then there are times I just need a hug and for someone to say...you will get through this.

Hospice. Initially, I really didn't understand all the services they provided. I heard about it briefly, but never had to utilize their services until **Crystal** had to be serviced by them. I had someone suggest that I have them service her in her home, but I really didn't feel right about doing that because I didn't want her children to have to see her body deteriorating daily. I didn't want them to have a visual of their mother dying right before their eyes. She went to a location that I will not name, but I was not pleased with them at all. They just wanted her to die (I know that's what Hospice does...they comfort the patient until their transition). However, I did not care for the nurse that was servicing Crystal. She didn't want to give her fluids or anything to help her live (I know...I was in slight denial at the time). She wanted to drug her up and let her die. I can remember that she even pulled me aside and tried to explain to me that my daughter was dying. Duh...I knew that! I didn't like it, didn't really want to accept it, but I knew it was going to happen (tears). The nurse was a little rude and not empathetic at all. Turns out Crystal had to leave that hospice care facility and be transported to the Providence Northeast Hospital for care. I was glad. It was at the hospital she grew to love (I know that sounds terrible because who loves being in the hospital, but they took good care of her there). She stayed there until her transition. It was there that this new Hospice company (the website information is listed for your convenience: https://www.nhpco.org/providers/heartstrings-hospice-2/) took care of Crystal along with the hospital staff. I was pleased with their service and care.

It Taught Me

I'm learning again that you can't rush the process. You must go through it completely but not get stuck in it. You must lean and depend on God for support when others are not around to lift you up. You can't rush the process of healing even if others around you want you to hurry up and heal and be how you used to be. I realize I will never be how I used to be. In the midst, God is changing me, pruning me, healing me, delivering me and perfecting those things that pertain to me so that I can impact someone else. Something good is coming out of this. I'm truly persuaded that it is. I just got to go through the process. No matter what happened between Crystal and I, through our ups and downs we experienced, I will ALWAYS love her.

Grieving with Grace

Sometimes people will want you to be how they remember you before your loss. It almost feels like a part of you leaves when they leave your life. The old norm no longer exists and now you have to live life differently. You can, and you will live through it and beyond it. Leaning on God and taking your time to grieve is necessary. Don't rush the process. Grieve, but heal too.

Did your family member have to go to Hospice? If so, how was your experience with them? If your family member had to undergo additional medical care for a length of time, share your thoughts in your journal.

Transparency Moment – October 21, 2019
A Chance to Love

Love. When it finds you and you find it, treasure it. She said, "I never really got a chance to love." Even though she had been in previous relationships, I knew exactly what she meant. She wanted to be in a relationship where she was loved and respected. My daughter, Crystal, made this statement one day as I was driving her back from Charleston after getting one of her treatments. I'm not going to go into too many details here at all, but there is so much to glean from this and what she experienced when it came to love.

It Taught Me
1) Love is kind. The Bible says so.
2) Love does not hurt constantly, nor is it abusive.
3) Any indications of red flags, yellow flags, green flags etc...it may not be love at all. As my daughter would say, "Don't do it." She often joked about me writing a book for her with this title regarding toxic relationships.
4) Love signifies value. When you love them, and they love you back...it means you value the one you are with.
5) When love finds you, really finds you, embrace it. Value it, treasure it, nurture it, respect it.

6) Don't let the toxic relationships that happened in the past cause you to connect with toxicity again or abuse love that is truly sincere.
7) Open your heart to love.
8) Forgive and love again. Forgive and love again.

Grieving with Grace

Love heals. It's the love and support of others that will help you through this new norm. Allow yourself to embrace the love of others to gain the strength you will need during this time.

Transparency Moment – November 1, 2019
Check on the Strong People

The other day I had someone ask me was I okay. We both realized that some people often feel as though strong people don't need to be asked if they're okay or checked on. I told her that I appreciate her for even asking and I appreciate those who have checked on me. Through this journey I've realized that some people really are concerned about my well-being, and they make it known by checking on me. So often we think that "the strong people" GOT IT. I've been so guilty about this myself. To some people, it appears as if everything is together, so they don't feel the need to even reach out to you. I have also found out during this journey of grieving that I've often needed people to simply check on me. When she asked me that question that day I answered, "I'm okay TODAY." I've come to realize that some days I feel so STRONG and other days those thoughts of my daughter, Crystal and the entire situation and our relationship flash before me and the tears, heaviness and occasionally some laughter (she was funny) come. I know the heavy emotions will lift as time progresses, but the impact of her presence in my life will never be forgotten.

After all, she's my first born. She came at a time when I KNEW NOTHING about myself or even about having a child. I was only 15 years old and oblivious to motherhood and all its responsibility. I can remember having to change her diaper while in the hospital and I didn't even know how to do that. One of the nurses had to show me how. I was sheltered and not groomed for motherhood at 15. When I said I KNEW NOTHING...I meant that.

It Taught Me

I've realized this too, that some people will never check on you. Even those you feel should, but that's okay too. I've come to realize that some people don't know how to communicate to those who may have suffered loss. They want you to continue as it was normally before the loss, but don't hold it against them. Either they don't know how to connect, or they don't care (oh my!). Or they may feel as though it's been a few months, so they think you should be okay by now, right? Yes, believe it or not some people are okay after a loss, but sometimes it's not the case for others and it takes them time to heal. It really depends on the relationship of the one they loss. No one wants to bury a child....no one. It's a different pill to swallow than when you lose a parent, grandparent, or an aunt/uncle.

However, I've also come to realize that even when we have encountered a traumatic experience, a loss, or an attack, we have the ability through the power of God to come through. Listen, there is no way I'm going to allow my daughter's loss to push me away from God or the plan of God for my life. I'm sure if Crystal could speak to me now she would probably say, "Ma, you better use those gifts God gave you and stop playing. For real, Ma you got mad gifts and ways to make money.... stop playing. You are bugging. Do what God is telling you." Yup. She and I would have these conversations. So, I know I've got to pull from the strength of God and keep going. I can't stay in captivity because God wants me AWAKENED (#AwakenHER). There is an assignment and God will get the glory out of all of this. I know He will.

Grieving with Grace

During your time of grief, when people check on you, be honest with how you are feeling at that time. Embrace the support and encouragement that they provide. Don't feel like you are a burden to them. If they are reaching out, it's because they want to assist you in some way.

And if you know others that are grieving along with you. Check on people. Even if they look like they are doing well and they are strong. Strong people know how to cover up the pain. They are strong. Your hug, your smile, your text, your conversation, your expressions of love are always needed by people. Believe me, I'm learning too. It's not going to take anything away from you to love someone today during their difficult times. Again, embrace the support that comes your way during this time.

Transparency Moment – November 12, 2019
The Drive to Charleston

Last year at this time I can remember Crystal being very sick. She wasn't breathing properly, and she wasn't clearly articulating her words. Some things she could remember and some things we just had to keep reminding her about. Around this same time last year, the home health nurse called for the ambulance to have Crystal transported to a local hospital because of her breathing and because she just was so weak. When I arrived at her home and the ambulance was there Crystal was fighting so hard not to go with them. Even in her weakest state, she still had that fight (LOL). She kept telling them that she didn't want to go to the hospital. She even said to me, "Ma don't let them take me. You are not going to let them take me." I was between a rock and hard place because I could tell she really needed assistance, but she just didn't want to go with them. One of the attendees of the ambulance talked with her and tried to comfort her but would not force her to leave with them.

However, the next day, I was instructed by the medical team in Charleston to bring Crystal to the hospital there. At this point she was willing to go. A part of her trusted the team in Charleston. I can remember her being very weak and having trouble breathing. She couldn't even remember certain things or people. It was as if she was going back to the infant stages. I drove her to Charleston, but I can remember one scary part during our drive. She had trouble breathing and I thought I was going to lose her on the way to Charleston. I can even remember yelling, "Oh God, I wish I had let the ambulance take you." (I was so scared I would lose her on that highway) She said, "Why....don't yell. I just need some water." I was so nervous, and I was asking God to help us get there safely. We made it to Charleston and when we arrived there we found out that Crystal's lung had collapsed and was filled with fluid (we later found out the fluid was even cancerous). She remained in that hospital until they called me in to give me the, "there is nothing else we can do speech." Just missing her today.

It Taught Me

No matter what we experience in life we must put our trust in God. When we've operated in our highest level of faith in God, we must step back and allow Him to fill in the gaps.

Even during Crystal's illness, she still had a fight in her to live. Don't be so quick to give up. Even if the odds are against you. Fight for your overall well-being and peace.

Grieving with Grace

When you start thinking about the events leading up to your loved one's death, you may find yourself trying to understand all that has happened. You may even begin to dwell on what you could have done differently. Of course you can't change anything now. Don't beat yourself up if you later realize something different could have been done for your loved one. You did your best at the time. As you reflect on those events and times with your friends or family members, write what you feel in a journal.

Transparency Moment – November 19, 2019
And She Loved You

"And she loved you." This was the text message response that I received from an old friend the other day. I was looking through some old pictures of a major event in my life and my daughter, Crystal, was in those pictures. I admired how her youngest daughter looks so much like her. I shared with that person about those pictures of her and he texted, "I know you miss her." I responded, "I really do. Even though we didn't see eye-to-eye all the time, but I loved her." His response was, "And she loved you." As I read the text it touched my heart in a special way.

As I look back, I know that I loved my daughter, and I know that she loved me. Through the years of our relationship that level of love was questioned on both our parts. Our love for each other had gone through some things that made it difficult at times to express that love, but it was always there. I remember one occasion when my daughter was in the hospital and she clearly expressed to me, "Ma, I love you. I really do love you." I responded, "Crystal, I Love You too." I was thankful for that day but wished we had expressed it more prior to.

It Taught Me

I glean from this: Love. Express your love to the ones that are in your life. Some of us grew up not hearing our family tell us that they loved us. Don't allow that to keep you from expressing your love to your spouse, your children, your family, your friends, and those that matter the most to you. Don't ever allow those around you to question your love towards them. If you love them, show them, tell them, make it known. Love heals. However, when people don't experience love from others they care about, it breaks them to a certain degree. When that love is shown during the darkest times...it can heal.

Forgive. Love. Forgive. Love. I'm not ashamed to say it, but Crystal and I wasted so many years because of her question of my love for her and then my question of her love towards me. But within our hearts we both loved each other. This is why I say, don't allow the pain of a mistake, misunderstanding, wrong action, derogatory words to break the cycle of LOVE. It's an old trick to create division in relationships. The enemy doesn't want relationships to overcome obstacles/setbacks. He likes it when there is division between a mother and her children, a father and his children, a husband and wife, friends that have known each other for years and so on...he wants to divide us all. STOP. Stop the hate, the bitterness, the anger, the division, and LOVE each other again. Spend time with those you love. Stop making excuses that you are busy, it's not enough time, you don't have the money, you got so much to do...STOP. Take the time to LOVE. Create happy new memories with those you love and with those who remain.

Grieving with Grace

As you go through your grieving process, reflect on the love you felt for the person you lost. Reflect on how they loved you. If there are some differences between you and your loved one, write them a letter to release your feelings about them. Share with them the things you were not able to say prior to them leaving you.

Transparency Moment – November 27, 2019
The Last Conversation

It's coming up to the first year since my daughter, Crystal, has passed away and I have mixed emotions. I can remember on Saturday, November 24, 2018, that Crystal sent me this message in messenger from her phone while in the hospital, "We s hranrdv ibhkkkkllmllllllkooo ok 9llllllllo0ooollllllllk ok o9olllllllllllllllloooo I am so I don't think."

I have no idea what she was trying to tell me because the cancer was doing its work on her brain. I didn't know how to even respond. It was getting to the point where we couldn't even communicate. But then something amazing happened and Crystal called me that same night and said, "Ma, come get me. I don't want to be in this hospital I want to go to Providence Northeast." Now this conversation wasn't clear, but I knew exactly what she was saying. I tried to explain to her that she couldn't leave without me first talking to the doctor (this was 3 days prior when they said there was nothing, they could do for her anymore). After I finished talking though, Crystal snapped back at me in her normal sassy way, "Ma, for real you not going to come get me. You not coming to get your daughter, really?" She hung up the phone. Now that was the last real conversation that she and I had. Three days later they would tell me there was nothing they could do, and they were not treating the cancer anymore. However, I'll have you know that Crystal spent her last days at the Providence Northeast Hospital like she wanted. Today, I remember her during this holiday season. I really wish I could have talked to her more that day. I know she is well, but I miss her.

It Taught Me

Spend time with family. Treasure those moments during this holiday season and days ahead. Let go of the unforgiveness and love!

Grieving with Grace

Connect with the other people in the family and see how they are holding up. Possibly consider some time together to talk or enjoy a special moment together. Holidays can be very difficult to maneuver through because you miss your loved ones. Connect with family and maybe implement something they enjoyed during your holiday season.

I must warn you that at times holidays are hard to get through. It appears the feelings of grief increase to the tenth power during those times. Prepare yourself for this. Talk with your family, friends and your therapist if you have one to get through it.

Transparency Moment – December 2, 2019
One Year Later

Well, today marks one year since my daughter, Crystal, passed away. This morning was a little tough for Jasmine and me. Jasmine had a hard time last night, but we're here. We are still standing...a little sad, a little teary-eyed, but we are still standing. This year really went by fast. The entire process has not been easy. I'm not even going to sugarcoat and say that it was, but I can honestly say, God gave me a strength I didn't even know existed. I miss my daughter so much and wish I could go back in time and change some things, but I know I can't. I thought I could get through today without tears, but they're coming anyway. I will never forget the call I got that Sunday morning to tell me that she had passed and then to go to the hospital to look at her lifeless body was tough. Then to look at her in a casket for the first time to view her body was even worse.

Then to walk down the aisle of the church (which seemed so long) to view my daughter's body for the last time on this side of Heaven was so tough!!!! The months of grief, sadness, denial, anger, days of going through my own personal battles in the midst of my grieving and even some days of laughter as I thought on Crystal. But through it all.... I'm still standing. And I remember my daughter on this day as being someone that loved her children, loved to have a good time, loved to make you laugh, cared for people, set people straight when you crossed her (yes, some cuss words would be released here and there....lol), she was determined, she was a hustler (had many talents), she was a dreamer, a true friend, a Christian. I remember Crystal during the time of her illness that she returned to God and to church. I can remember quite a few times Crystal_shouting in church and doing her dance before the Lord at the altar. We shouted together and for that I am thankful to God. She made it into Heaven and that is my consolation. She left me with something. something that I must do to bring glory to God and to help many others who suffered just like her. God will get the glory.

It Taught Me

Sometimes when we suffer loss, or we go through traumatic situations and/or opposition, we feel as though we won't make it through that point. Or we even ask ourselves, where do I go from here? (I know I asked that same question this same time last year). It's evident now to me that you keep going and you keep living with a new norm. You get a better understanding about life and the things that really matter. You process through, you seek God for counsel, comfort, and direction. You push yourself through. You lean on those who are stronger than you until you become strong yourself.

You cannot change yesterday. You can't, but you can change how you allow it to affect you today. I thank the Lord for allowing Crystal to be a part of my life. There is so much I've learned.

Grieving with Grace

If you are approaching another annual year of your loved one's death, think about some of the good memories about them. What are some of those good memories you can reflect on today? Take a moment to journal them down. Take some time to talk with others about them. Are you planning to do anything in their memory (balloon release, special dinner, reminiscing about the good times shared)? I want to encourage you to keep pushing forward you're doing good.

Transparency Moment – December 3, 2019
The Emotions Resurfaced

Today is a better day. I must admit, yesterday was hard. I honestly thought that I could get through the day and do my daily routines, but to my surprise that was not the case at all. I will forever love and remember my daughter Crystal. She is a part of me. Yesterday, I experienced a different part of the grieving process. The feelings and emotions that I felt a year ago began to resurface. It felt as if she had just died...again. I can't explain it...those who have experienced loss can identify. All I wanted to do was cry and get in the bed. I had to leave work because I just couldn't get it together. It was tough, but today I'm much better.

Sometimes you may not know how you're going to get through a tough time or even a tough day, but you must realize that you will get through it. Even though you may experience some pain, tears, disappointment, some frustration or whatever the emotion is, you will get through. The key is to not remain there or allow yourself to get entangled in emotions. You must keep moving to the best of your ability.

It Taught Me

I know I've repeated this numerous times but lean on God. Through this journey, I have literally learned about the power of God's strength. His strength is truly made perfect in our weakness. I am a witness!!!

I learned something yesterday. You need to recognize when you are not as strong as you think. Yes, strong people get weak. Strong people hurt; strong people get angry, strong people need to cry sometimes. Check on your strong people, they need love and hugs too. Someone shared with me yesterday that they realized I needed to be strong for so many. She then asked, who has you covered when you don't feel as strong? If you don't feel as strong sometimes, that's okay. Really...it's okay. This helps you to recognize that you need God's help. This helps you to recognize that you need to tap into your support system. You need the comfort, prayers, and strength of others to build you up until you are strong again. And yes, you will be strong again.

This may sound crazy, but it's true, Crystal's death is teaching me so much about living. Take care of yourself and live. Enjoy life to the fullest (she did it). Have fun. Enjoy and love your family and friends. And don't wait on doing what God assigned for your hands to do. Do all you can for God beginning in your youth, beginning right now. God needs you.

Grieving with Grace

If you feel as though you need a break, or need to step away to regain your strength, do so. Don't push yourself too fast through the grieving process. Take your time. Sometimes you may need some time off. Take the time you need. On the day of their birthday and the day of their passing, you may have to take time off from work if you start feeling overwhelmed. Don't feel bad for doing that. Do what you need to do, in a healthy way, to get through those days. Our body is known to keep the score if it has experienced trauma. Losing a loved one can be traumatic so take your time through the days ahead.

Transparency Moment – December 18, 2019
The Release

As I look back and reflect on this month, my emotions seem to be all over the place. Last year this time it was very sad for me because of the loss of my daughter, Crystal. It was truly a tough time. Something I would never wish upon anyone, not even my enemy. Losing a loved one is tough. Losing a child....is even tougher, but I can honestly say God has provided a strength that is unexplainable. Regardless, it was not easy by no means and at times it is still very tough. Earlier this month as the date of her departure from this side of Heaven arrived (12/2/18), I thought I would be able to get through the day a lot better than I did. The first thing I remembered was having a very detailed dream. God was making me aware of some things around me. I went to work, but I had to leave...it was just too much. Tears were coming, but the day ended well. I made it through and I'm grateful.

Throughout this year I've had the time to process her loss and how it has impacted me. There are still some things I must continue to process.

Through it all, I believe God is up to something good. I recently went on a cruise (Hen Gathering) and I thoroughly enjoyed myself, but initially it was bittersweet because I kept thinking about my daughter. On the cruise there were a few mother/daughter teams. When I saw them, I thought of Crystal and me. My daughter and I had talked about going on a cruise together prior to her chemo, but it didn't happen. I thought of her and wished we had done that together, but at times, while on the cruise I felt like she was there. During our prayer time on the cruise, I really got an opportunity to release some things - even pertaining to the pain deep within that I yet still feel. The release letter activity that we had to do on the cruise was so powerful. I cried so much after I tore that paper up and placed it in the bowl. I gave it to God.

I miss my daughter very much, but I'm thankful that God has kept me through this process. I'm still standing and something good will come out of this.

Thank you to everyone that has encouraged me through this year. There are books, community projects and speaking engagements coming out of all this. There is a Kingdom Assignment attached to this and I know God will make it clear. I miss you, Crystal.

It Taught Me
Create good memories with those you love. God will use a setback to create your comeback. You are coming out of silence because you really have something to say.

Letting go of and releasing yesterday's regrets is a must because you can't change IT, but you can create good days NOW.

Grieving with Grace

Take the time to write a release letter to your loved one. Share how you feel about your life now since they've been gone. Share anything else you wished you could have told them.

Transparency Moment – January 17, 2020
Thoughts

I miss her, but sometimes I just don't want to think about her. I know that may sound strange, but there are times that I think about my daughter, Crystal, and it creates so many different emotions....and not all of them are happy ones. There are times that I think of my daughter, and I begin to remember her pain. Thoughts of being told by the doctors that they wouldn't be doing anything else to treat her cancer. Thoughts of her being transported from Charleston to Columbia praying that she would stay alive so that her children could see her one last time. Thoughts of the call from the Hospice nurse telling me that she had passed away. Thoughts of how I felt the day I had to walk in the funeral home and view her body for the first time. Thoughts of walking down the aisle of the church to take one final look at my daughter on this side of Heaven. Thoughts of seeing them lower her body in that casket and closing it shut. Whew! My God.

So sometimes I don't want to think about her because it is still so shocking to me that a person so lively could be shut down so quickly. I know there are good memories, there are good times and times we were so closely connected. I remember those times too, but sometimes I just don't want to think about it at all. I can remember last night looking at her picture that's on her obituary.

All I could say is, "Goodness…. Crystal, I can't believe it!" I know I can't pack down my feelings and hide them under a rug. I know I've got to release them and allow God to continue to mend my heart from this. Believe me, God is really helping me through this all. As I thought about her last night, I realized I didn't cry as I would have normally done. I even realize that the tears aren't coming now when I type this and usually, they do when I write these transparency moments. I then began to realize that a portion of that pain was left on that ship when I went on the cruise in December 2019 with the Hen Gathering. I can remember at one of the sessions when we had to release some things that I cried so hard that day. I mean I cried like it had just happened. I believe that day a part of me released it. I was able to release some of the pain. Now that doesn't mean I don't love my daughter or that I will forget her, that will never happen. It just means that I'm releasing the pain of her loss to God (oh boy, the tears coming now). If I stay in that pain, I won't be effective. I'm purposing in my heart to do something big in honor of my daughter. My prayer is that God will guide me and help me to do it. (Wow, I thought I was going to make it through this writing without crying).

It Taught Me

It is so important to release to God what can seem so unbearable for us to handle. God knows all about it. Let it go...release it to HIM. Cast your cares upon Him because He cares for you. It's too heavy for you to handle. Give it over to God and tap into your support system.

When you stay in your pain, in your past mistakes, or continue to dwell on your shortcomings, you then lose your ability to be most effective. There are lives that you must encourage on this journey so you must be strong enough to help create change in their lives to the glory of God.

Grieving with Grace

Through the grieving process so many different thoughts are going to race through your mind. Some of those thoughts will make you sad and some may very well make you smile...even laugh as you think about your loved one. Process your thoughts, journal them if you like and possibly share your thoughts with a friend or a therapist if you find yourself struggling through this thing called grieving.

Transparency Moment – February 3, 2020
When is she coming back?

I must admit these last few days I have had a lot of thoughts concerning my daughter, Crystal. I miss her and so do her children. We are all maintaining in our own way. I know Jasmine had a tough time this past week. Thoughts of her mom sparked conversations. I tried my best to encourage her as best I could. I also took some time to share with her what I wanted to do in honor of her mother. Then this weekend we had the twins spend the night. Sometimes it's hard to be in their presence because of our loss, but I realize we all need to stay connected. As I was riding in the car taking the twins to my house they started talking about their mother. First, they asked about the car I was driving (which was my dad's, but he gave it to Crystal first and now it's my youngest son's car). Kymani asked whose car it was and Keoni quickly responded, "It's our mommy's car, but Poppy gave it to her." He's so smart and such an old man in his young age. Then they wanted to go by their mom's house (the last place she lived) and I said we can stop by there tomorrow. Going there is still a little tough sometimes.

Then I asked, "Do you miss your mom?" (I already knew what the answer was).

They both responded, "YES!!!"

Kymani asked: "When is she coming back?"

Me: Blank stare. My mouth fell wide open....and I didn't know how to respond.

Keoni: "She's not coming back. We'll see her a long time from now." (I told you he was an old man. He saved me because I didn't know what to respond). I really admire Keoni's responses. He's so smart. I'm sure Crystal would be proud of her two little people.

It Taught Me

It's moments like these that I wish the outcome for Crystal was a whole lot different, but I know there is nothing I can do about that, but a whole lot I can do for her children and advocating for those like her.

Even though you may be okay, there are still people around you that may not be. Use whatever strength you may have to help them through so they can get stronger.

Grieving with Grace

Acceptance is the last stage in the five stages of grief. Sometimes it takes a while to reach the point of acceptance concerning your feelings about your loved one. However, you will need to get to the point of acceptance to truly move through life in a healthy way. Accepting it doesn't mean you will forget about them, or you'll never think of them again, but it means you are moving forward with life as best as you can.

Transparency Moment – June 12, 2020
Don't Burn Bridges

She's still on my mind and in my heart. The other day I rode by the last house she lived in. Not sure why. I know she isn't there, but maybe it was just a point of contact. A couple of weeks ago, I befriended a good friend of hers on Facebook and when I saw his profile picture I threw my phone down on my bed. It was a picture of my daughter and granddaughter. Oh, how I wish my daughter was here. I know we didn't always see eye-to-eye, but the love was there.

Sometimes outside people try to interfere and tamper with the love you have for another. Sometimes people get jealous of how you love someone. They don't have a connection with anyone, and they don't want you to have one either. Love people anyway.

It Taught Me
Don't let ANYONE break a bond with someone you love (healthy love) someone you've connected with that has helped you in some way. Don't burn bridges that you may later have to cross. Some people want to separate you from the ones you love only to isolate you for themselves (unhealthy). If you have a daughter, if you have a son...love them. Treasure that relationship, build it strong and love unconditionally.

I think I rode by her house as a point of contact, but to also show her.... I got a new car. I know it sounds strange, but that's what I sincerely felt.

Grieving with Grace
Sometimes the loss of a loved one brings people back together, possibly even restore relationships. Don't burn the bridges and/or don't allow the bridges to burn anymore. Be open to restore some relationships within the family that might have been estranged prior to the loved one's passing.

Transparency Moment – January 21, 2021
Friends

This is about my father who passed away on December 27, 2020. He and Crystal passed in the same month, two years apart.

I really miss my father. He was such a good man. Every time I go in the kitchen and look at the seat he used to sit at the kitchen table, I think of him and wish he would come downstairs and ask for the milk out the refrigerator (He drank a gallon in two days...literally. Crystal warned me about that, but I didn't believe her at the time until I saw it for myself).

One of the things I admired about him in his later years was his connection with people. He truly was a light to many. Whether he just talked with you, shared some humor, or gave some encouraging words to help you to keep going...it brought light. Every day he would make several calls from his phone (flip phone actually) to his friends and family members. The conversations weren't long, but they were made. One of his friends told me that they had been friends for over 80 years (and my dad was 87 when he passed). That is so amazing to me.

It Taught Me

Connections with people (friends, family etc.) are so important to maintain. It's important to stay connected and check on each other. In this day and time, we are so quick to text, inbox, but find it difficult to pick up the phone (Facetime, Zoom). I've been guilty of this myself. This is something I'm going to work on. Through all those years, my father stayed connected to those various people that he talked to on a daily/weekly basis. Amazing. Now, I know they may not have seen eye-to-eye all the time, but they didn't allow that to block their connection. We shouldn't allow offenses to keep us from staying connected especially if it can be resolved. Love and forgive. Check on someone today.

I love my daddy and I'm sorry to see him go. I'm a daddy's girl from my core. My dad, my mom and Crystal are having a good time in Heaven. Now it's time for me to allow my LIGHT to shine here and continue the work that God has purposed for me to fulfill. Lord, help me to be a light....

Grieving with Grace

When processing your grief, it's always good to hear from those that love and support you. It helps to push you through and at times will provide some strength to move through the new norm. Who were the people that were there for you during this time? How have they been a help to you? Possibly reach out to them and let them know how much you appreciate their love and support.

Transparency Moment – January 22, 2021
Be a Light

Yesterday I was thinking about my dad and this scenario came to my mind that took place when I was a little girl. I remember we were coming home from grocery shopping) and we were about to walk into the apartment that we lived in at the time. My dad was carrying a grocery bag, and I can remember looking up at him and saying, "Daddy, I want to marry you when I grow up." Now that speaks volumes; especially now.

There must have been something I saw in him at the time that prompted me to say that out of my mouth. Now, I know I couldn't marry my father, but something about him made me say that. I think most girls look for qualities of their father (especially if you had a good one) in their future mates.

It Taught Me
People need to see the good in you. It's important to discipline ourselves so that good character and God's expression of love shines through us. I saw something that day in my father that I wanted without even realizing what I was saying.

Be a light that others would enjoy being around. Be a light for God that others would be drawn to Him. Be a light so that other individuals would say, "I want that for my life too."

Grieving with Grace

Someone has been a light for you. Who was that? Share about the people who have been a light for you. In what way was your loved one a light to you? Reflect on the lessons you learned from them and write or share what you feel about those lessons.

Transparency Moment – February 2, 2021
The Kitchen Table

Yesterday when I came home from work, I paused at the door when I first walked in. I did that because I saw the kitchen light on that was above the kitchen table. I immediately thought....my dad is sitting at the table. I had to catch myself because I knew he was gone. Just to hear him say, "How are you? How was your day?" or "Pass me the milk out the refrigerator." - would be a joy to hear. Missing him and still sensing his presence.

It Taught Me
Sometimes we take for granted the relationships we've established and their impact on our lives. Treasure the ones that you love. Tell them you love them. I know love is an action word and all, but some people in your life need to hear you say, "I Love YOU!" Honor, respect and value your parents. I miss my daddy. I'm a daddy's girl for life!

Grieving with Grace
What are some characteristics about your family members that you miss the most? Take a moment to reflect on this and journal about it. What are some of their favorite sayings? Share those favorite sayings with those you know or other family members.

Transparency Moment – February 5, 2021
I'm Okay

For the last couple of days, I've been thinking about my father and his last days at the hospital. There was a point during his illness where I couldn't visit with him, but I was able to Facetime him to see how he was doing. I knew he wasn't doing well, but I was hopeful and prayerful that things would turn around for him. When I would ask him how he was doing and then I'd tell him I loved him, he would always say, "I'm okay. I'm alright. I love you." Even down to the last day that I was able to hear him speak, he said it. "I'm okay."

It Taught Me
I believe when he said it, he believed it or wanted it to be so. I honestly don't know what he was thinking at the time, but I believe he really wanted to be okay. You know when we're going through tough times, we often blurt out how we feel instead of what we really want it to be. My father always tried to keep things positive, so I believe he wanted to continue doing so even while preparing to transition.

I believe he said it to keep me calm. Maybe in his eyes I was still his little girl that he had to protect and to make sure I was okay. It was a sign of strength to reassure me not to worry about him because he was and would be okay.

As I was discussing what happened to my dad with a friend, another perspective was brought to my attention after discussing what happened to my dad. My friend asked me how I was doing, and I said, "I'm okay." And they said, "No you're not." They said, "You're saying exactly what your dad said, but in actuality he was not okay (Healthwise)." At that moment, I had to admit, I was not okay.

Sometimes we are not totally honest about what is happening to us, what we're feeling or what we are perhaps dealing with. We tend to cover up our pain, hurt, disappointments and our need for deliverance for the sake of another (I guess) or to avoid embarrassment (I'm not sure). When we're not honest (authentic) about what is happening with us, the healing stagnates. The breakthrough is halted. The pain, the hurt, the feelings of being disappointed and the feelings of grief are prolonged.

Grieving with Grace

Sometimes you may not want to feel the feelings of grief. Sometimes you may want to avoid or push the feelings aside. You may even tell others that you are okay when you're not. I say that to say this: If you're not okay, be honest about it and get some help to heal so that you can really and truly be okay

****

This writing also marks the date of my mother's passing on February 5, 2005. Another day I will never forget and the days leading up to it. January 31, 2005, the fire in the house took my mother's life. She didn't burn in the fire, my daughter Crystal was able to pull her out of the bedroom, but she waited in the bathroom for Crystal to return. Crystal took the girls out of the house and wanted to return, but when she tried to, she couldn't go back in because the fire was still happening. The fire continued to blaze until the fire department arrived and were able to go back upstairs. They found her unconscious in the bathroom. She was in the hospital for a few days, but she breathed too much carbon monoxide and suffered brain damage and had to be taken off life support. Something my father did not want to do but had no choice. I remember her today as well. Mommy, I'm so sorry.

Transparency Moment – February 15, 2021
Valentine's Day

A special memory for me. Yesterday was Valentine's Day and many people have their opinions as to whether it should be celebrated or not. To each its own. I remember Valentine's Day being special while growing up as a young girl. My father would make sure my mom, me and Crystal got something (usually candy or a stuffed animal - sometimes money; usually a flying $20 bill). My mother gave to my father as well, but my dad made sure all of us had something. I agree that love should be shown every day to those that matter the most in your life. Love is an action word. So, a special day set aside to show your love.... never hurt anyone.
Keep on LOVING!!!

It Taught Me
Show love to people you care about. Having a set time or any time to share your expressions of love is not limited to one day but should be shown in some way.

Grieving with Grace
Were there special occasions that you and your loved one shared? Reflect on those special occasions today. Journal your thoughts if you like or share with another friend or loved one.

Transparency Moment – February 18, 2021
The Telephone Call

You know what? God is so amazing. He knows exactly how to encourage you. Just as I was typing about missing my dad, my father's secretary called on my father's phone (yeah, I still got it on). She couldn't remember my number, so she called on his phone. Sometimes it's hard to talk to people that knew the ones you loved. You just don't know if the tears are going to fall or what. Well, this conversation lifted my spirit because she shared some of the funny stories that took place in my father's dental office. I appreciated it so much. It put a smile back on my face concerning my father. He was a good man and he liked to laugh.

It Taught Me
Love people and laugh more. LIVE!!!
Sometimes the conversations we fear to have could very well be beneficial to us in the long run. Create new and enjoyable memories. And take time to reflect on all the good times you've had. Be thankful.

Grieving with Grace
Try your best not to avoid talking to those who have a connection with the loved one you lost. Sometimes those conversations can help you get through to another day. Talking about the good memories you all

experienced with your loved one can have the capacity to brighten your day.

Transparency Moment – February 18, 2021
Missing Him

I miss my daddy! I sensed him this morning when I was praying in the house. I kept thinking I need to be a little quiet, so I don't wake him. Soon realizing that he wasn't there. I know he's okay, but that doesn't mean I don't miss him. I miss Crystal too! I wish I could tell her some of the things that are happening now. I know there would be a lot of laughter. Sometimes I must remind myself that I am not alone.

It Taught Me
Love. Enjoy your life. Love others. Treasure moments together with those you love. Smile. Laugh more.

Grieving with Grace
Days of missing your loved one are going to happen. It's part of the process because you loved them so much. They played an important part of your life and when that part is missing it can be difficult to move forward. What are some things you miss about them the most? If they were here now, what would they tell you? What are some of the things you would tell them now? Reflect on these questions and write in your journal.

Transparency Moment – March 3, 2021
Grieving with Grace

The other day I was on my way to church and thoughts of my family ran through my mind. As I was driving, I started having feelings of being alone. I couldn't help but think that the people I loved and started out with before moving to SC were gone. My mother (2/5/2005), my daughter (12/2/2018) and now my father (12/27/20). Wow! I can remember that right after my father died, I wanted to go back to NJ (I know...it sounds crazy because I have family here), but I guess I just missed the old times after burying my father that day. They are gone and at times it really makes me sad. I even began to question God as to why. I'm not bitter or angry. I just miss them all. I know God has a plan for me and I'm willing to do what He's called me to do. I know that they are well and I'm sure they are rooting me on to keep pressing.

It Taught Me
I've learned some valuable lessons from all three of them. I've learned some things about myself. I'm learning how to cope. I'm learning how to continue to do what God has purposed for my life. I'm learning how to pull from the strength of God. I'm finding more and more each day that the Lord is the strength of my life.

I can remember someone telling me after my daughter died that I had to realize that I was alive. She may be gone (they may be gone), but I'm still alive. And with this life I have, I will give God glory and praise. I will utilize the gifts He gave and be a source of encouragement to those in need. There is work for me to do and I'm willing to do it.

Grieving with Grace

Grieving is a process. It's not something that can be rushed to heal from. It takes time and everyone's experience is different. Believe me, at times you are just fine and then there are those days that you remember the ones you loved, and it brings different emotions. Today is one of those days. I miss them all.

Listen, while you are grieving the loss of a loved one, allow yourself time to heal. Release the pain. Know that you did the best you could for the ones you loved. If things weren't resolved, forgive yourself...forgive them and move on. **#grievingwithgrace**

Transparency Moment – March 16, 2021
At Midnight

Last week I was planning my birthday celebration and before going to (logging on) my virtual party I couldn't help but think that my dad would not be in the house to wish me a happy birthday. I would also be missing his famous "flying $20" bill as he called it. I had been waiting to receive his final death certificate since his passing in December 2020. Come to find out it finally became available the day before my birthday. I just so happened to pick up his death certificate on my birthday (March 12). I was okay.... sort of. I love my daddy and I miss him so much. He was indeed a good man. He brought strength, balance and stability to me.

When I looked at the time of death on the certificate it said 0000. I asked what that meant. I was told he passed at midnight. My God. When I walked out of the funeral home, I thought about that.... midnight. So many things happen at midnight. I remember hearing sermons about midnight. How things seem hard, and it may seem impossible, but at midnight things begin to turn. In Acts 16:25 - even though Paul and Silas were entrapped in prison, at MIDNIGHT they began to pray and sing praises to God. I believe my daddy had a MIDNIGHT experience as he left this side of Heaven to be with his Creator.

It Taught Me

Listen, you too may be going through some hard times and need some consolation. Know that things change at MIDNIGHT. Things are about to turn for YOU! Weeping may endure for a night, but joy comes in the morning. Let praise be in your mouth and rejoice in knowing that this too shall pass!

Grieving with Grace

You will soon find out that dates, times and places may trigger feelings of grief as you remember your loved one. As the anniversary day of your loved one's passing approaches you may feel some emotions as you go through your daily life routines. It's like your body remembers that time is coming. Once again, feel the feelings, talk with someone, write out your thoughts. This will help you to manage through those feelings and emotions

Transparency Moment – April 14, 2021
Granddaughter

I am so grateful for an opportunity to be able to spend some time with one of my granddaughters on our spring break. It was such an amazing time and she hung with me the whole time. Usually she may visit other people, but this time she stuck close. And I loved it. We got a chance to really talk about her future and her goals. She is such an amazing young lady, very smart and full of wisdom. My daughter, Crystal, her mother would be proud of her. Being with her brought some bittersweet thoughts. I felt Crystal and my dad strongly in our midst.

It reminded me of how my daughter, and I used to be together all the time. When you saw me, you saw Crystal. When we moved to South Carolina...things changed. Some of the things that happened often play back in my mind and I often think about how I could have handled some things better. And I believe some things could have been handled better by Crystal as well, but I realize I can't change the past. All I can do is learn from it. When history tried to repeat itself, I found myself responding differently.

I appreciated this time with Jasmine. Our connection helps us both to heal from our loss. We lost Crystal, but we gained each other. I can continue to love my daughter through her. I know I've shared this before. I remember when Crystal was going to put Jasmine up for adoption. She already had one daughter and she felt it would be difficult to take care of another child. When she was in the hospital, she hadn't even held Jasmine. We had the adopted couple ready, but something within me rose up and I went to the hospital and told Crystal, "You can't give her up." I called the nurse to tell her to bring Jasmine in the room so that Crystal could hold her. You see, I must have had a flashback from my past because I was going to give Crystal up for adoption (my parents suggested it), but when I held Crystal....I knew I couldn't do it. I was only 15 years old. When Crystal died, Jasmine was 15. Crystal and I didn't get a chance to do that mother/daughter trip that we talked about, but I'm glad she had an opportunity to take that trip with Jasmine.

I hate that my daughter is not here. Oh, my goodness, there is so much I want to tell her. There is so much I wish I could have said or done (I'm not living in regret. I forgave myself a long time ago). There is so much we could be laughing at right now. Crystal had a way of making a tough situation funny. I miss that.

When my granddaughter leaves for the military I will truly miss her. I know we will stay connected, but I'll miss her being around. Lord, help me because that's going to feel like another loss, but I'm excited about her future. I know that she will do well.

It Taught Me
Spend time with those you love. Invest in people. Sometimes it's not with the money you give, but the time you make to create meaningful experiences with others. You can't change the past, but you can forgive others and forgive yourself. You can learn from it and when a similar scenario arises, respond differently. What you do has the ability to create change.

Grieving with Grace
Spending time with those who knew and were connected to your loved one may be helpful to do. There may be children, grandchildren, nieces, nephews, aunts, uncles, cousins and friends. Keep the connections. Sometimes the connection will help you all to heal through the grieving process together. Reach out to them and stay connected.

Transparency Moment – April 20, 2021
The Triggers

I know that I shared about this before, but it happened again. Sometimes when we've experienced loss or have undergone a traumatic experience there are certain triggers that take place to remind you of the incident and/or the experience. Sometimes the triggers will move you into tears, anger, feelings of depression or whatever emotion that surfaces. Yes, I know we can't be led or moved by our emotions, but sometimes triggers do just that and they come out the blue. Well last night and last week I experienced some triggers.

The one last week occurred after someone sent me a song called, "Alright, OK" by J. Moss. Really nice song and uplifting. I started playing it, but then I saw the words, "Alright, OK" and I immediately thought of my father and the tears came. Boy, did they come down like someone had turned on the water faucet to release water that had been backed up for some time. The person that sent the song meant well, but those two words took me to another place. I started thinking about my father in the hospital closer to the latter days of his life. I would always ask him how he was feeling and doing, and he would always respond, "I'm okay. I'm alright." I knew he wasn't. I wondered did he know he wasn't. He just kept saying it each time. Staying positive in the midst of losing his life. I guess he also said it to me to keep me calm as well. I knew he wasn't alright, and I knew he wasn't okay, but I appreciate him saying it.

It's good to keep positive amid whatever struggle we may be experiencing. Sometimes it's the very words that we say out of our mouths that help us through our process and journey through life. I knew my dad was trying to remain positive. I hated to see him that way. I felt helpless. A person that had done so much for me, I wasn't even able to help him during this part of his sickness (I wasn't allowed in the hospital at a certain point). The only thing I could do was keep talking with him and praying for him. I know he's well, but I miss him.

The second trigger came late last night as I was doing some studying. I was looking at information about the unconscious mind. I thought of the time when my father was unconscious and was drifting from life to death. I asked to speak to him via Facetime to see if I could call him back. I said, "Daddy, daddy...can you hear me?" No answer. He was crossing over to glory. I had to fight to hold back the tears last night. As I said, I know he's well, but I miss him. My daddy was such a good man and I appreciate all that he did for me and for my daughter and grandchildren. I honor him today.

It Taught Me

If you're not okay or if you're not alright, it's best to let someone know. First, tell God about it! He loves you so much and wants to help solve whatever has you troubled. Then seek help if you need it. Sometimes we need someone to lean on that understands what we are going through to help us along. I want to encourage you by saying: You are resilient. You are doing a good job. You will make it. You will get through this.

Grieving with Grace

Triggers are going to happen. You may not be able to stop the triggers, but you can try to control its impact on you. Sometimes you can prepare yourself and sometimes you just can't and that's okay. Take time to identify your triggers and then identify ways to help yourself move past them.

Transparency Moment – April 27, 2021
Go by the House

"Believe me, I get it." This is what I said to myself this past weekend when I had my twin grandchildren with me this weekend. Kymani asked me to take her to go see her mother's house. She wanted to go by to look at it. Well, she wanted to go inside the house. She wanted to see her old room. She wanted to see her mother's room. She wanted to see if her toys were still there. I get it. She wanted to go back to a place where she remembered some happiness with her mom. She misses her mom and she talked about her while she was with me. I can remember a few years back I got an opportunity to go back into the home I was raised in. At the time, I felt just like Kymani. I wanted to go back to the place where everything started, where I felt the love and the support, that safe place. I was so appreciative of the new owners that allowed me to walk through that home...my home. It will always be that for me.

So, I told Kymani we can go by her mom's old house, but I didn't know if we would be allowed in. When we got in front of the house, Kymani said just ask if we can go in. Well...you know what happened next. I went to ring the doorbell and explained to this stranger that my granddaughter and I needed to come in or at least look in her house. As I write this...it seems so crazy. The lady was hesitant, but she allowed us to at least stand at the door and look in the house. I held Kymani's hand as I watched her look inside. I said, "Are you okay." She said, "Yes." I thanked the woman, and we went back to the car. Kymani said she was glad to at least see the house, but she understood she couldn't go in. She's so smart.

I believe Kymani got some closure. I believe she just wanted to go back to a place where she was happy. A happy place where she had memories of her mom. Oh, how I wish Crystal was here to see her two little people, but they are doing well. I know she is watching them from Heaven.

It Taught Me
It's good to be able to go back to some places and reminisce on good times, but those experiences are in your past and you must move on from them. They played a prominent part in your growth and development, but because you change, people change, and things change you can't always physically go back. Good memories are always stored in our minds and resurface when we need comforting the most.

Sometimes you must be bold enough to go after what you want. Even if it looks and sounds crazy to others...your inward witness will tell you to push forth. I believe Kymani has tenacity.

Grieving with Grace

It's okay to reminisce about your experiences you once shared with your loved one. Those good experiences will always be a part of you. Hold them dear to your heart and treasure them. If some of the memories have not been so good, try not to entertain those thoughts, forgive and move forward.

Transparency Moment – July 14, 2021
Trip to New Jersey

I realized on this last trip to New Jersey that there are still some things I need to process and things I needed to release myself from concerning my father's death. Boy did I cry in that hotel room! I had to use a therapeutic method, "the empty chair." There were things I had to tell him about how things happened during his hospital stay until his last breath and how he looked after passing. I miss him so much. There is an emptiness I feel that I really have to ask God to fill. Sometimes I feel so alone, but I know I'm not, but the feeling is real. They all left me...

However, I must remember God kept me. He has me here for a reason. I'm alive and well! It's for a purpose. It's for a divine plan and there is an assignment I must fulfill. Ultimately, I want to do what God has called me to do. I'm appreciative of His grace.

It Taught Me
Time to heal. God has equipped me with many gifts, but I recognize there are some areas that I need time to heal. In my healing process, God will build, rebuild and strengthen me for the rebirth!

Allow God time to do what He needs to do in YOU. He does so well with the formulation of masterpieces!

This post may sound like it's full of emotion because it is. Grieving is emotional at times, but God knows how to stabilize you. I've learned from my daughter, Crystal's passing about the importance of leaning on God for strength. He's bringing me through it all for HIS glory.

Those hidden things that still need healing, allow God to mend. Allow time to mend. Doing so will benefit you and everyone else around you. When you rush through the process it can become detrimental to your overall wellbeing.

May God's peace be with you TODAY!

Grieving with Grace
Time to heal. Allow yourself time to heal. Grieving is hard and because of that you can't rush through the process. What are some things that you are still struggling with? What are the areas in your life that you still need healing from? Share and write about your thoughts concerning this.

Transparency Moment – August 3, 2021
Moving Clothes

I think I'm on my healing pathway. The other day I gathered some of my father's clothes out the closet and put them in one of the local clothes bins. I had to make sure I checked those pockets again because the last time I checked I found close to $500. Listen, my daddy used to stash money around the house when I grew up.

I thought I would be in tears, but I pushed through. I miss him dearly. I'm a daddy's girl from the heart. My daddy was a good man, and he was good to me. I appreciate his love that he shared with all of us.

Now, I still have to go through Crystal's things. Yup...going on over 3 years (at the time this was written) and I still have some of her shoes and items from the house. I think part of me is still stuck in 2018. I'm getting better though. It is still unbelievable that they both left in the month of December two years apart.

Love is forever. And I know the song says forever is a long time, but that's how much I'll love them all.

It Taught Me
You must release and let go of things that serve you no more purpose.

Grieving with Grace

It may be difficult to get rid of your loved one's items. It will pull you emotionally so you may have to prepare yourself to go through and get rid of their items. Do it in segments of time and get some help if you need that. It's not as easy as it may sound to be. You may think you're just going to go through the items and discard them. However, you will find that some of those items will stir some emotions. Take your time.

Transparency Moment – August 20, 2021
The Comments

I can remember the looks. I can remember the comments. After my daughter passed and even after my father passed, I began to lose weight. It was noticeable to me, and it was noticeable to others. Some would look me up and down. Some would say, "You are so skinny. You lose a lot of weight." Little did they know, it used to cut me when they said it. I wanted to say, "Ummmm....in case you didn't know my daughter died.... you would lose weight too!"

I'm sure some of them were thinking, "Is she sick too?" At one point the whole thing troubled me. Behind closed doors it would really upset me, but I would try my best to smile. I had every test I could think of to make sure I was in fact alright. I prayed. My husband prayed. No cancer. Just dealing with the stress of losing loved ones and being on the wrong medications. The loss of my loved ones caused me to lose weight. Some people gain weight when dealing with stress and trauma and some lose. Some people go through other means to deal with loss, grief, stress, trauma etc. It's important to be empathic and understand a person's feelings during the grieving process.

It Taught Me

In essence, when people are dealing with loss, grief, stress and/or trauma they are affected in many ways. Sometimes it's in their physical body, sometimes it's in the emotions (mental health --very much so), health and/or how they interact after the trauma. Be patient with people, love them through it, encourage them, help them if you can. Be mindful of your looks and your comments because it could be those things that can take them over the edge with depression or it could help them get through their struggle. Take a moment to encourage someone today.

Grieving with Grace

Take care of yourself. Don't be moved by people's comments. I'm convinced that sometimes people don't know what to say to people who are grieving. Sometimes people don't even know what to do. You may have to give some people grace and don't allow it to upset you. Additionally, if they continue to upset you, let them know how it makes you feel. Help them to understand why it does and how they can help you as you move forward.

Transparency Moment – September 6, 2021
First Day of Chemo Memory

I remember this day so well. Thursday, September 6, 2018 was my daughter, Crystal first time for chemotherapy in Charleston at MUSC. I remember that day how we talked, laughed and slept during the time she was getting treatment. We enjoyed each other even during a tough time for her. That day changed our lives completely. The chemo was too harsh for her body. She fought as long as she could. There have been numerous times that I wished things would have turned out differently...today being one of those days

It Taught Me
Some things in our lives we may have wanted to work out in a different way. Sometimes we may not understand why things happened the way they did. We wonder if we could have done things differently. Going over shoulda, coulda, and woulda is not going to solve anything at this present time. Sometimes you have to accept that you did what you could at that time.

Grieving with Grace
As time moves forward, you are going to remember certain dates such as birthdates, special occasions and even the day of your loved one's passing and you may

experience some emotions. As I said before, feel the feelings. Talk with someone about it if you need to.

Transparency Moment – September 7, 2021
God Still Needs You

On Friday, September 3, 2021, I was walking through my living room to get to the kitchen and the Lord dropped something in my spirit. I had been thinking about the loss of my daughter and my recent loss of my father and I was feeling a little heavy. Then the Lord spoke something to me. He said, "Yes they are gone, but you're still here and I don't want to lose you." My God. I stood still. He said, "I don't want to lose you." In other words, God was letting me know that yes, your loved ones are gone, but I need you to be present. God has more for me to do. God is fully aware that it hurts, but I can't allow myself to become so sad that I become depressed, stuck and lose sight of what I must do for God.

<u>It Taught Me</u>
Maybe this is for someone else too. You have suffered the loss of a loved one and yes, it hurts. Yes, you will cry sometimes. Yes, at times you will even feel depressed, angry, lonely and helpless.... but you're still here. God wants you strong. He wants to still use you. God can turn your pain into power. God needs you (let that sink in). Allow God to strengthen you so that you can strengthen another. All I can say is, "God, help me to help those that cross my path."

Grieving with Grace

All I can say is that you are still alive. Because of that there is still a purpose for your existence. You are not done yet. You can't give up on you. You must keep going. Keep living. I know it's hard, I truly understand, but you've got to find whatever bit of strength you have and push through this. You may have to change the way you do things, to prepare you for a new way of living, but you can do it. Your loved one would want you to continue living your life.

Transparency Moment – December 27, 2021
Daddy, You Did Well

Last year on this same day, I lost someone I truly loved. He loved me, took care of me, provided for me and protected me. This day and the days prior to his passing were so difficult. So many emotions from that day until now have crossed my mind. Why? Could something have been done differently? Did I make the right choices concerning his care? How could the hospital be so negligent? My dad went in for one thing and caught COVID IN THE HOSPITAL! Every time I think of that it upsets me. I am praying about that.

But one thing I can say about Earl Garrett, Jr is that he was a good man. He inspired many people along the way. As he worked in his dream job of dentistry, he got an opportunity to not only do what he loved but he met so many beautiful people along the way. He loved to talk, tell jokes and make you feel at ease.

At a young age, my father lost his mother, but he pressed through. When my mother passed away, he missed her dearly. They were high school sweethearts. As a matter of fact, while he was in the hospital he even said. "Marian called me." I froze when he said my mother's name. I was like, "Tell her you can't talk to her." I guess God was trying to tell me something then...

However, after her passing, I noticed a strength in my father...he kept going. He kept living! I know he missed her so much. I'm sure he got his strength from God. I will forever love my daddy always and eternally. Daddy, you did well!

It Taught Me
I know I have mentioned this numerous times throughout this book, but I must share it again because it's the truth. Through tough times, we must lean on God's strength. God's strength is made perfect in our weakness. The times that we feel the weakest is when God places His strength in us and around us. He will surround us with people that will teach us how to continue to move forward. Someone around you is teaching you something that you may need now and in the future. Glean the wisdom from them. Learn and apply it. You will experience a strength in your life you never thought you had.

Grieving with Grace
So many times, after losing those we love, a part of us stops living, we get stuck and some of us don't want to continue. But you have to keep going. You must keep living. Those that have gone on would have wanted you to do so. God's strength is made PERFECT in your weakness. Draw from the strength of God and keep going. Keep living because so much more awaits you.

GRIEF FACT SHEET

Grief hurts, but it can be helpful. The process of grieving often involves sadness, anger, loneliness, and other painful emotions. However, grieving can help you come to terms with loss and move forward in life, while still cherishing memories of your loved one.

Everyone grieves differently. Although others may have opinions about how to grieve correctly, your grief is yours and yours alone. Some people need to express their grief, while others prefer to process in silence. Some feel anger, while others feel sadness, numbness, or relief. Everyone has different reactions to loss, and different needs during the grieving process.

Grief does not have a set time frame. Grief can last for weeks, months, or years. It may come and go around holidays, anniversaries, and major life events, or it might always be in the background. However, grief does tend to lessen in intensity over time.

It's okay to seek help. Support from family and friends can prevent grief from growing out of control. Although grief will improve over time for most, this isn't always the case. When grief is especially debilitating or long-lasting, support groups, therapy, and other resources may be beneficial.

Moving on doesn't mean forgetting. You can continue to live your life, have new experiences, and form new relationships, while continuing to love the person you lost. The goal of grieving isn't to forget, but rather to figure out how you would like to remember, while moving forward.

**Provided by Therapistaid.com

Stages of Grief

Denial: An attempt to protect yourself from an upsetting reality. You deny a loss will happen, minimize your feelings about it, distance yourself from people who have accepted it, or refuse to talk about the loss or your emotions. You may feel numb or disconnected.

Anger: A way to express pain or fight against a difficult reality. You feel angry or enraged at yourself or others. You may lose your temper easily, lash out, or blame others.

Bargaining: An attempt to control or prevent the loss. You beg and plead for the loss not to happen. You might tell a partner you'll do whatever they want if they stay with you or try unproven treatments for a terminal illness.

Depression: A reaction of sadness or devastation that shows the loss weighs heavily on you. You feel hopeless, crushed, or a sense of longing. You might cry and isolate yourself from others. You might be unsure how to move forward.

Acceptance: A processing of the loss—even though it remains painful--and a gradual movement toward a new normal. You accept the loss logically and emotionally. You might recall good memories, talk about your grief, or even find meaning in the experience.

**Provided by Therapistaid.com

About the Author

Stephanie L. McKenny is a native of Montclair, New Jersey. She received her license to preach in August 1993 in Newark, NJ. She assists her husband in the ministry where she serves in various capacities. Stephanie McKenny has three children and four grandchildren. She is a graduate of Columbia College. She continued her graduate studies at Webster University for a Masters in Mental Health Counseling. Stephanie L. McKenny is a Licensed Professional Counselor in Columbia, SC. She is the author of over 10 books. Her latest book is: ***"GOD NEEDS YOU UNSTUCK."*** Stephanie McKenny can be contacted via email, website and social media: slmckenny@gmail.com, her website address is: www.stephaniemckennny.com. She is also on Facebook, Instagram and TikTok.

If you would like to book Stephanie L. McKenny for a speaking engagement, book signing, workshop/book discussion, you may do so by emailing her at: slmckenny@gmail.com.